What People Are
'The Silent

"*I first found out about Helen's work when she was nominated for and subsequently won Best Healer in the Health & Happiness Awards. My heart was warmed by the wonderfully touching testimonials from many of Helen's clients. This resulted in me having high expectations of this book – and I'm pleased to say it was every bit as enlightening as I expected it to be.*

If you have suffered or are suffering psychological abuse in any relationship, this is the book to read. By sharing her story, Helen enables you to identify patterns of abuse in your life. It then opens your heart and gives you the tools to empower yourself. The result: you are able to stop damaging patterns and bring the cycle of psychological abuse to an end. Helen shows you that you CAN live a happy life and enjoy loving, healthy relationships."

Sarah Derrington ~ Co-founder, *Health & Happiness Magazine*

"*From a therapeutic perspective, I feel this book reflects the lives of so many I work with; echoing the thoughts, feelings, emotions and behaviours, experienced by survivors of abuse. Explaining how low self-worth directly affects the attachments we make, and takes us on a journey travelling from victim consciousness, to self-realisation. Personally, Helen is a great inspiration, grounded, whole and an incredible woman, who I am proud to call a friend. I admire her strength and courage to re-visit her past in order to help others.*"

Jayne Wheeler ~ Independent Sexual Violence Advisor & Counsellor

"If you have been struggling with abuse, whether emotional or physical, this is the book to read. By bravely sharing her story with the reader, Helen shows that you can free yourself and release the pattern of abusive behaviour in your life. Not only does she disclose her own experiences, but she also reveals how the reader can empower themselves and take ownership of their present and future."

Pennie Munslow ~ Author of 'The Circle of Life'

"Out of a path of domestic violence it's great to read a spiritual journey with help & guidance for a person's self-healing."

Terri Rutter MBACP, DipHypno ~ Self Help Coach

The Silent Sufferer

Helen Courtney

The Silent Sufferer

Copyright 2015 © Helen Courtney.

www.evolvingyou.co.uk

ISBN 978-1-907308-10-9

First published in Great Britain by Compass Publishing 2015.

A catalogue record of this book is available from the British Library.

Set and designed by The Book Refinery Ltd.
Edited by Danielle Wrate.
www.wrateseditingservices.co.uk
A 'Hearts of England' collaboration.

Helen Courtney asserts the right to be identified as the author of this work.

Illustrations by Holly.

This is a work of non-fiction. The events and experiences detailed herein are true and have been faithfully rendered as the author has remembered them, to the best of her ability. All names and identifying characteristics of certain individuals have been changed in order to protect their identities.

My Dedications

To the numerous victims of psychological abuse
around the world; I dedicate this book to you.

I graciously gift this book to our present and future generations, who I
believe are our ambassadors for change. I am confident that through
awareness, courage and, most importantly, united action, abusive behaviour
will be proactively ousted from the shadows and into the light.
Together, we CAN and WILL make abuse a thing of the past.

I trust this book will assist you in some way during your own inner journey
of self-discovery, and in reclaiming your personal power, so that you can
shine bright like a diamond!

With love, gratitude and joyful blessings always,

Helen

Acknowledgements

I offer my sincere and heartfelt thanks to all those who have supported me in writing this book. First of all starting with my two amazing children who are my greatest teachers and continued inspiration in life.

To my loving husband; thank you for supporting me on my journey and helping me to trust humankind again. Thank you also for recognising my true worth and for encouraging me in my career.

To my amazing mother who has always been, and continues to be, my rock. I love you dearly and I am incredibly proud to call you 'mum'.

To my oldest and dearest friend of twenty three years; thank you for being there for me through thick and thin. Thank you also for your continued support and friendship, and for gifting me your time and expert eye on this book.

To my newest friend Angel Alison; my deepest thanks for inspiring me and making me accountable for finally writing my story.

To my clients and students; you have shown me just how strong and courageous the human spirit can be during times of transformation. Also, thank you for affirming the work I so dearly love and enjoy.

Contents

PART ONE

Contents

PART TWO

Contents

A Note From The Author

Every person has a story to tell and I am no different. This book was born out of my own personal experiences of psychological abuse in my relationships with family and friends, as well as at school and in the workplace. I understand the long-term negative effects that abusive relationships have had on my beliefs about myself and others, the choices I've made and the life I have lived. I've been on a twenty-year inner journey of transformation and I am delighted to have turned my negative beliefs into positive ones so that I am:

- Comfortable in my own skin.

- Confident about my abilities.

- Able to value and respect myself.

- Able to live life authentically in line with my values.

I wrote this book to raise awareness of psychological abuse in today's society, and to share my experiences and the knowledge I gained along the way. I also want to highlight the many natural healing practices available that allow the soul to heal itself of past emotional and mental wounds, gracefully facilitating lasting inner peace, happiness and abundance. I trust that this book may therefore help others who may be struggling in some way.

My own personal transformation motivated a change of career and I retrained in various healing modalities to finally become an Self-Realisation Expert.

What is a self-realisation?

In its simplest form, self-realisation is the fulfilment of one's potential. This sounds easy doesn't it? In reality however, self-realisation happens over many years and requires effort, as it encompasses self-mastery. Through self-mastery we can break through any self-imposed restrictions or conditioned limitations such as ego patterning, break free from mental limiting beliefs, habitual negative behaviour and ancestral programming. We take personal responsibility for all areas of our life so become free from external coercion, worldly attachments and playing the blame game. We become TRULY free to co-create with the laws of the universe, the life we want and deserve in order to fulfil our life purpose.

Over the years I have worked with many men, women and children from different socio-economic backgrounds, religions and walks of life. I have helped people with a variety of challenges such as addiction, panic attacks, relationship difficulties, career worries, grief, confidence issues, fears, and the extensive list continues. My clients came seeking help for specific issues, so it didn't initially occur to me that there may be a common thread in the challenges they faced. Over time however, I noticed that many had an unconscious contributing factor to their current challenge; psychological abuse.

For many, abuse is automatically associated with domestic or sexual violence. However, this is a common misconception as abuse takes on many forms, including mental and emotional cruelty. Through my therapy work, I discovered that many people at some point during their lives have suffered from some form of psychological abuse from either family, friends, or at school or work. In numerous cases, clients didn't necessarily identify the other person's behaviour as abusive at the time of occurrence. The psychological abuse suffered by clients created unconscious mental and emotional wounds which had long-term negative effects on their self-worth, ability to make healthy decisions, beliefs, behaviours, and their lives as a whole.

In most but not all cases, clients had suppressed the past incident for differing reasons, some of which are outlined here:

- They were too young to fully understand it at the time.

- Psychological abuse was commonplace in their world.

- They had become accustomed to being treated that way.

- They believed it was somehow their fault.

- They were ashamed.

- They excused the behaviour as being carried out in jest.

- They didn't want to accept that the abuse happened.

When I established my business *Evolving You*, I originally worked as a Transpersonal Therapist and clients came for healing as the techniques I used were highly effective at transforming their past physical, emotional or mental wounds. Clients were more than happy with the positive changes that were occurring as a result of our work together and regularly recommended me to family and friends. However, there was a part of me that felt my clients needed and deserved more than a healing session.

My *'eureka moment'* came at the end of clinic one day, when I recognised that my work was in fact disempowering my clients. I was mortified by this revelation. When I started working as a therapist, it was my intention to connect people with their personal power, teach them to trust their gut instinct and to always offer them choices in order to honour their free will. So I questioned how I had allowed my practice to become disempowering. Upon reflection, the answer was evident.

People attended therapy sessions in order to heal some aspect of themselves, so they were indirectly stating *"I want you to fix me please"*. By virtue, they were also giving away their personal power and so denying their innate ability to self-heal. Over the years, I have realised the importance of a client's participation in their own healing journey. Treatments which deny clients the chance to embrace and take full personal responsibility for their growth devalues them as individuals.

On my quest to create a safe, nurturing space for clients to heal and experience free expression, I had unknowingly denied them the opportunity to fully participate in their healing. Clients thanked me for the healing I provided, when in reality, I was merely facilitating the healing for them. I had unintentionally allowed myself to become a rescuer and a crutch to my clients. I unwittingly allowed and unconsciously encouraged them to stay in victim consciousness, which went against my own core values and beliefs. I knew that if I was to continue my work authentically, I had to change the way I connected and worked with clients.

I spent valuable time reflecting and intuitively evolved my work to combine the already successful healing techniques with new mentoring methods. I became my own 'guinea pig' so that I could trial them and experience the results for myself. As a kinaesthetic learner, this way of working made sense to me and was a natural extension of my personal journey.

After reflection, adaptation and trial, I implemented a new collaborative way of working with clients and it proved to be highly successful. My clients felt empowered to take personal responsibility, were held accountable for their development and became their own best resource in times of stress or during personal challenges. Partaking in Self-Realisation sessions enabled my clients to transcend their life story by healing their physical, mental and emotional wounds. Our work together highlighted to me:

- The delicate relationship between our physical, emotional and mental bodies.

- The power of the subconscious mind.
- The control of the ego.
- The influence of self-sabotage.
- The significance of our inner child.
- The importance of our core values and beliefs.
- The significance of connecting with our resourceful state.
- The ability for individuals to transcend their story.
- The intrinsic relationship between our past, present and future.

I was incredibly impressed at how quickly and effortlessly people embraced this new way of working, and how mentoring blended so naturally with the healing aspects of my work. I continue to use this approach with my clients today, as I feel for reasons previously explained, that healing alone isn't enough for people to permanently evolve beyond their challenges. I also believe that mentoring alone isn't adequate either, as it fails to address an individual's unconscious energy blocks which have accumulated over their lifetime and which are often deep rooted and incredibly restrictive.

I believe that a client's feedback is the true testimony as to whether a method is effective or not. I experienced a continuous flow of positive feedback and referrals, so I knew that I had a winning formula. Clients remarked that they appreciated my clear explanations and 'no jargon' approach, which helped them gain a greater understanding of themselves. People also thanked me for enabling them to feel relaxed and for providing a nurturing space for them to be themselves in, without fear of judgement.

Clients observed that the knowledge gained during therapy sessions helped them achieve a deeper understanding of themselves and that with this came a greater appreciation of others. Many made a conscious decision not to be so judgemental of others, as they realised that when you meet someone for the first time, you only see them at that particular moment in their life and are therefore unable to comprehend or fully appreciate their life story and the wounds they may be carrying. Once we become more accepting, patient and tolerant of ourselves, we extend this same gratitude to others, and vice versa.

When we understand ourselves at a deeper level, value ourselves, honour our values and live authentically, I believe that we experience true inner peace, happiness and fulfilment. Many gurus, world and business leaders know this already and it is this wisdom that I am passionate about sharing with my family, friends, clients, students and readers.

Today, I am less affected by life's challenges and dramas. That is not to say I am unaffected by them, as I am living a human existence after all. When I feel that I have said something unsuitable or behaved inappropriately, I remind myself of the 80/20 rule. I believe that it is impossible for someone to be perfect 100% of the time; because if it was possible then surely we would be a saint or Buddha. There is always room for further knowledge, growth and evolution, but life is about experiencing the full spectrum of emotions and events, so that we can learn to live consciously and authentically.

Clients and students regularly used to ask me if I had written or recorded any material that they could work with at home. My reply was always the same, *"Sadly no. Not yet anyway."* So to those people who asked me that question; this book is partly because of you, thank you for gently nudging me in the right direction and having the confidence in me to create such a book. I guess this book grew from demand rather than my personal desire to be an author.

Emma Watson (the actress who played Hermione in Harry Potter), during her speech to the UN at the *HeforShe* conference said, *"If not me, who? If not now, when?"* When I doubted that I was capable of doing justice to a book on abuse, I watched Emma's conference speech on YouTube as encouragement. If we as a nation are to change abuse, then we all have to unite. Sufferers with the right knowledge and professional support ARE capable of transcending beyond victim consciousness. Together we CAN highlight the inappropriate actions of physical and psychological abusers so that they take responsibility for changing their patterns of behaviour. If we allow abuse to continue in this generation, then it will also carry on in the next. I for one do not want my children to grow up in a society where psychological abuse is 'the norm'. If abusive behaviour is allowed to continue, then why would abusers want to change?

"I wanted to change the world. But I have found that the only thing one can be sure of changing is oneself."
~ *Aldous Huxley*

My daughter introduced me to the above quote when she was just eleven years old. As individuals, I believe that we are ALL capable of healing our own wounds so that we can clearly see our TRUE worth and value. From a self-realised mindset, we can create strong, healthy boundaries concerning the way we show love to ourselves and are loved by others. Living consciously and through a sacred heart we can BE the best version of ourselves that we can possibly be, and therefore change the world.

I have done my best to make this book as user friendly as possible, making information concise and chapters short.

Part One of this book is my life story and is written from memory and my journal entries. I have written from my personal perspective, sharing my feelings and how I saw events at the time. To protect my family and friends all names have been changed, as I feel individual identities are irrelevant to the story itself. What is important is the information contained within the story. This highlights:

- The cycle of abuse.

- Victim mentality/consciousness.

- Every challenge can be overcome.

- Life is a journey full of opportunities for personal growth.

- Every situation can be healed.

Part Two of this book contains key information which I regard as my medicine and fundamental in my journey from victimhood to self-realisation, as it allowed me to have a broader understanding of myself and relationships. Whilst Part One of this book is my story, I would like you to regard Part Two, as *yours*. In order to facilitate your personal journey through reflection, understanding and change, I recommend that you engage *honestly and openly* with the questions and statements that I have asked. These have been specifically designed to help you connect with your inner most thoughts and feelings and identify areas for healing.

It is my intention for this book to be an educational resource helping others who have been, or who are in, psychologically abusive relationships. Whilst the wounds of physical abuse are visible to the human eye and heal over time, the scars of psychological abuse are unseen, run much deeper and can last a lifetime. The cycle of abuse is a debilitating one, and is the main cause of low self-esteem, poor self-worth, depression and unhappiness. As we can't *visually* see the scars of psychological abuse or its effects, it makes it much harder to identify. We can't physically see the air we breathe with the naked eye, but that doesn't mean that air isn't real, right?

Denying that psychological abuse has or is happening does not change anything, nor does it make it stop. In fact, quite the opposite, as avoiding the reality of psychological abuse gives it power and allows it to continue. I believe the first step to change is awareness, as awareness leads to freewill choice. By making educated choices a person can either decide to:

- Remain stuck in their old pattern, going around in circles and living their life on repeat, like the movie '*Groundhog Day*';

- Make changes which offer opportunities for healing, growth and transformation.

It is my wish that through this book, my training and one-to-one programs, I will start a positive evolution revolution. It is my hope that in the not too distant future, schools recognise the importance of the mind-body-spirit connection. Wouldn't it be fantastic if our children learnt about the power of the subconscious mind, the significance of core values, the power of words, being authentic and living from a sacred heart? Wouldn't it be wonderful to live in a self-realised society with individuals co-existing in peace and harmony in a world without fear?

With love, peace and joyful blessings,

Part One

My Story

The Tipping Point

"Stop shouting at each other, please stop shouting, you are killing me,"** cried Drew. He was curled up on the kitchen sofa with his hands tightly cupped over his ears to block out the noise of his parents yelling. This wasn't the first time Drew had witnessed his parents aggressively arguing with each other. Sadly, he and his older sister Freya were regular and unwilling spectators to the persistent rows that took place in their home. However, the venomous spat that morning was one too many for Drew to bear; it was his tipping point.

Quarrels and disagreements had become the 'norm' in the Evans household over the years, but recently they had grown in frequency and intensity. In fact, rows were no longer reserved for behind closed doors or confined to the household. There were now uncomfortable public displays of verbal differences, whenever and wherever. The 'happy couple' public image had started to lapse and it was apparent that the relationship was far from loving or joyful. A male friend had recently commented: *"Are you two incapable of having a normal conversation? Can you hear the way you talk to each other? Think of the kids!"* Sadly, it was true; My husband and I were incapable of having a civil conversation with each other, even for the sake of our children.

On that cold winter morning in February 2010, Drew, a usually quiet eight-year-old boy, who loved playing and having fun, found his voice. In that poignant moment, he had concisely expressed his thoughts and it was evident by the veracity in the way he spoke that he meant what he said. His deeply repressed feelings dramatically gushed out of his mouth, like lava erupting from a volcano. His painful words resonated around the room and were heard crystal clear.

The pause button was pressed and time stood still in the seconds that followed Drew's eloquent outburst. In that brief moment, it was as though someone grabbed my shoulders, looked deep into my eyes and yelled, 'wake up'. It was like being roused from a dream, or should I say a nightmare, but the reality was that this was not a nightmare that I could wake up from. Every day I suffered and endured the horror story of my existence. However, that day presented me with the opportunity to face reality and change my life story.

The play button was pressed and time resumed. My awareness returned to the room and in front of me I saw Drew lying on the sofa crying. Seeing my vulnerable little boy in emotional pain instantly shattered my heart into a million pieces. I knew that it was my choice to stay in a hurtful marriage, but my children had no choice at all. I lovingly embraced Drew with a warm and secure hug, as if sticking a plaster to a wound. I told him that I was deeply sorry, promised him all would be okay and then reassured him, as I always did.

My apology was heartfelt, sincere and genuine, as I was sorry for much more than just this latest incident. I felt remorseful that Drew and his sister had to listen to regular disagreements, that they seldom saw their parents show any kind of affection for each other and rarely enjoyed family days out. The reality for Freya and Drew was that although their father and I lived under the same roof, we both led separate lives. Their father used the excuse of work to come home late and would always find a reason not to go on family days out, which was incredibly hurtful. I often felt like a single mother, taking them on days out or weekend breaks on my own, when all I wanted was for us to be a family.

When I promised Drew that everything would be okay, I wanted more than anything in my heart for my words to be true. I longed for a happy marriage with a loving, stable home for our children, but in order to create that I needed a committed husband to help me. I couldn't comprehend how it would be possible considering our differences of opinions and inability to communicate.

For the time being, I would have to be satisfied that my words and love would be sufficient to dissolve Drew's pain and pacify him. However, as a realist, I knew that any comfort I offered would be temporary. The cracks in my marriage were evident and were so deep that they were beyond repair. Over the years, I had tried everything to fix my dysfunctional relationship and marriage, but sadly to no avail.

After easing Drew's hurt, it was time to do what I always did. I sucked in my pain and put on my mask of pretence, which secretly hid my true thoughts and feelings from the outside world. I wore this false persona so habitually that I could no longer identify with the real me. The real ME was dead, buried and long gone. I was an empty shell living life in a zombie-like state; numbed by years of heartache, disappointment and psychological abuse. My mask was my reliable protector, trusted friend and my only means of getting through each day.

I suddenly became aware of the time and noticed it was against us as school was about to start. Drew and I gathered our belongings, made our way to the car and I drove us to school. After successfully completing the school run, I had the necessary space and time to reflect on the stressful events of the morning. Drew's words and actions were so powerful that they had stopped me in my tracks. I owed it to my children to awaken from my state of denial and be willing to confront the reality of my marriage and life.

Regrettably, Drew's words and actions had no effect on his father that day. In fact, I felt as though they didn't even register and believe it's fair to say that Robert successfully ignored that morning's incident and just got on with his life by going to work. I made a conscious decision that this latest event would not be brushed under the carpet with the other ugly truths of our marriage. The carpet bulged at the edges with sixteen years of eluded issues, repressed emotions and unvoiced conversations. For Robert, avoidance of marital issues was always favoured over confrontation, but that morning I pulled back the carpet to reveal the unsavoury reality of our marriage.

Over the years, I had developed specific coping strategies in order to survive, but seeing my child's heart aching was more than I could bear. Like Drew, I had reached my tipping point and for the first time in my life, I temporarily stopped the sixteen year roller-coaster ride of mixed emotions and multiple dramas. I willingly removed my rose-tinted spectacles and assessed my life objectively with detached emotion. For my own sanity and for the wellbeing of my children, I had to make the most challenging decision of my life; a choice which could change family life forever. To make that decision it was necessary for me to look back over our relationship and revisit my painful wounds.

2

Once Upon A Time

My love story began when I was just eighteen years old. I worked as a part-time receptionist at the local health club, which provided me with an income, whilst studying for my A-Levels at Sixth Form College. It was an ideal job, as my complimentary gym pass permitted me to stay physically fit and the social aspect provided the opportunity for me to widen my friendship group.

It was there that I met a twenty-six-year old, 5ft 10" body builder and civil servant named Robert. He was a member at the gym, as well as the best friend of one of the owners. Everyone knew Robert and he was exceptionally popular with both men and women. He was 'one of the lads', referring to every male as mate and he was extremely charismatic with the women, often participating in flirtatious banter. At eight years my senior, with a muscular physique, piercing blue eyes, a cute smile and a self-assured exterior, he was out of my league.

After working at the club for a while, I decided to treat my mother to a gym session to help with her fitness. Upon arrival in the reception area, Robert eagerly introduced himself to her and then proceeded to express his views on how wonderful he thought I was. His introduction was socially polite, as you would expect when meeting someone for the first time, but it was what occurred next that surprised me. He continued by informing my mother that he would marry me one day, which stopped me in my tracks. His words were surreal and actions bizarre, as we weren't even dating.

After work, I would often go to Robert's house to enjoy a take-away meal, watch a movie or go to the local pub for a drink. Our friendship grew over time and as a friend, Robert presented himself as the perfect gentleman. I began to see a different side to Robert to the one he portrayed in public, and my initial impression of him as a womaniser was beginning to change. He was kind, thoughtful and considerate with a vulnerable and needy side. Although I didn't believe that he would be romantically interested in me, I started to experience feelings for him and so began to drop my guard.

Then one evening, Robert surprisingly asked me out on a date. I was both shocked and pleased, whilst also feeling very apprehensive, as although I had seen a different side to Robert, deep down I knew that he was a player at heart. I tentatively agreed to go out with him, pre-warning myself to be careful and to simply view the evening as two friends enjoying each other's company. I was more than aware of Robert's compelling nature, so I was cautious not to be seduced by him in the same way other women had been. I most certainly did not want to be added to his long list of heartbroken casualties.

We had a thoroughly enjoyable evening at the local wine bars and as we were both already friends, we were very relaxed in each other's company. Our first date came to an end and Robert asked me if I would like to see him again. He had previously expressed to me on numerous occasions that his player days were behind him and he was ready to find the right person to settle down with. Therefore, I thought to myself that I didn't want to miss the opportunity of being his 'Mrs Right', and despite my reservations, we started dating.

Our relationship developed quickly and within the first few weeks of dating, he introduced me to his parents who were kind and generous. They embraced me readily into their family and we soon enjoyed Sunday lunch each week at Robert's family home. I was happy, content and felt incredibly blessed to be dating such an amazing guy.

We valued a balanced blend of nights in together as well as nights out as a couple or with friends. I was completely smitten and our relationship felt so right. I was obviously wrong to doubt Robert when he said that he was ready to put his bachelor days behind him and settle down. I had been unfair judging him on his past, as most people decide to settle down at some point in their life. Maybe Robert just hadn't found the right person before?

After dating for several months, Robert's behaviour started to ring alarm bells, but I chose to ignore my gut instincts and carried on as usual. He asked me not to tell anyone at work that we were dating, as he was a private person and didn't want everyone knowing his personal business. This seemed reasonable so I concurred. Later, I discovered that the genuine reason for his request was that he wanted to maintain his single status at the health club. This allowed him to legitimately flirt with other women at the centre without any of them being aware of the other women he was seducing at the same time. In fact one day at work, I overheard a woman telling her friend about a date she had been on with Robert. I knew in my heart that she was talking about my Robert but convinced myself that it could be someone else, despite the fact that there wasn't another member called Robert at the centre.

Robert also expressed that he didn't like to hold hands in public, as he was not a particularly tactile person. I later learnt that the actual reason for this was to preserve his public single status. That way he could state that he was out with a friend if seen with myself or another female. Another of Robert's requests was that

I did not approach him when he was on a lads' night out. Every Friday night, Robert would go to the local wine bars, where my friends and I also socialised. Robert made his wishes quite clear, with the excuse being that it would be unfair on his friends if he spent time with me whilst out with them. I later learnt that this was another ploy for Robert to retain his single status in public and provided him with a cover story. Robert led two separate lives; one with me, which provided love and security, and the other which provided danger and fed his ego. Robert was happy to enjoy the best of both worlds, which allowed him to have his cake and eat it, so to speak.

I stupidly ignored the signs. Why? The fundamental answer to that question was that I loved him. I was deeply in love with the part of Robert which offered me affection and attention. He was charming, fascinating and loveable. I allowed Robert to continue to coerce and exploit me, wanting and believing his plausible excuses to be true. I assumed that whilst we were dating our relationship was exclusive, however I was unwise to make such assumptions. In reality, Robert dated several women at the same time on different evenings, which explained why he would only see me on Wednesday and Saturday evenings, and Sunday daytime.

Maybe there was an element of Robert that wanted to grow up, settle down and have a family in order to replicate the happy marriage of his parents. After all, he had quickly integrated me into this family. Robert's brother had two young children who stayed with their grandparents every weekend, so Robert and I helped out by taking care of his niece and nephew when we could. We enjoyed taking them on day trips, to the cinema, shops or restaurants.

During our trip one day to the Sea Life Centre, Robert asked if I would have my photo taken with him, his niece and nephew. He said that he wanted a memento of the day to put up in his home.

Robert's request totally surprised me, as his home was a typical bachelor pad, with no family photos on display at all. I agreed, so we had our photo taken with the huge model octopus at the entrance of the centre. Later that day as we walked around, Robert said to the children, *"we like Auntie Helen don't we?"* to which they both replied, *"yes"*. He then asked them, *"do you think Auntie Helen should move in with Uncle Robert?"* to which both children gave the same positive answer.

I looked at Robert in amazement and he swiftly asked me to move in with him, promptly followed by his wish that one day we would get married and have children of our own. My brain didn't have time to think before my mouth responded to his question with a huge smile and the word *"yes"*. After all, why would he ask me to share his home if he wasn't serious about our relationship? Maybe he hadn't been serious about our relationship until now? Had my brain engaged in any reasonable level of thought, I would have said no and continued dating him, but I was falling hook, line and sinker…for his lies.

3
Wounded Soul

At eighteen years of age, I was 5ft 7", underweight at just eight and a half stone, and had blonde hair and brown eyes. I was short-sighted, so despondently had to wear glasses, which knocked my self-confidence. Being underweight, I was always body conscious about being less voluptuous than others my age. I wore a mask of self-confidence to hide my insecurities, as well as my lack of self-belief and worth.

When Robert and I met, I was a wounded soul who was naïve and vulnerable. I was naïve due to my age and inexperience of life and vulnerable due to the emotional wounds of my childhood, my mother and father's separation and even my conception. My life began during a New Year's celebration in 1974. I was the result of an unplanned pregnancy; my mother and father had no plans to conceive more children, as they already had one child and had lost another.

Growing up my mother would constantly reassure me that I was the best accident that ever happened. However, my father viewed the unexpected pregnancy very differently, as his lover had also fallen pregnant at the same time that my mother conceived me. My father demanded that both women terminate their pregnancies. His lover obeyed his insistent request, but thankfully my mother refused. I think that may have been the first time my mother stood up to my father and I am extremely pleased that she found the courage to do so. I have my mother to thank for giving me life in more ways than one.

I am unsure if my father was pleased with my mother for continuing with her pregnancy. I know now, however, that he wanted a male heir, so he was disappointed with the news of another daughter on the day of my birth. Whilst growing up, I was blissfully unaware of my father's desire for a son, although interestingly there was always a part of me which felt rejected by him on some level. I loved the pretty dresses that my mother handmade for me, but a part of me grew up as a tom boy. I would prefer to socialise and play with boys rather than girls, as they were less whingey, easier to understand and consistent in their behaviour. I relished my time with my boy friends, as we would go on adventures, bike rides, play hide and seek, make dens and play curb ball. Boys didn't mind getting messy, either. Some days, to my mother's despair, I would play in the street gutter collecting stones, which I stored in jam jars under the telephone table in the hall at home. To this day, I can't understand why I did that, but I remember it being great fun.

When I was very small, perhaps only three or four years old, I recall happily playing with my toys in the living room when I heard my father return from work. I ran out into the hall to greet him with a hug. Whilst I squeezed his legs as tight as my little arms could manage, my father just stood there with his arms by his side. He was unable to reciprocate my affections or demonstrate his love to me.

In stark contrast to my father, my mother made me feel wanted, loved and safe. She would spend hours playing with me, baking cakes and taking me on walks to the park. She read fantastic bedtime stories, sang to me and took me to dance classes every Saturday. It was obvious how much she enjoyed being a mother to my older sister and me. She kept our home immaculately clean, always ensured we were well fed with a two course home-cooked meal every evening and dressed us beautifully. She showered us with lots of hugs and affection, maybe as a way of making up for the lack of affection we received from my father.

The feelings I experienced whilst growing up, combined with my inner knowing, drove me to continuously seek my father's approval and love. I never felt good enough for my father as a child and the effects of this extended into other areas of my life, as I would incessantly seek the approval of family, friends, teachers and boyfriends. This inner desire for approval adversely affected my self-esteem, beliefs about my self-image and how I related to people, especially men.

At seventeen, I learnt why I felt rejected by my father. After copious amounts of questioning my mother finally gave in and told me the truth about my birth story. I was initially angry at my father for treating my mother so badly, disappointed that I had such a selfish father and then I finally felt relieved. At long last my inner feelings had been validated and I finally understood my inner desire for approval from my father, as well as from others. This knowledge, however, didn't give me the tools to change this unhealthy pattern of behaviour, so I continued needing affirmation from others.

Only now, after years of therapy, can I objectively reflect back on my childhood. I understand that my relationship with my father is a karmic one which has taught me:

- I do not need outside approval.
- The importance of self-approval and love.
- That you can't make someone else love you, no matter how hard you try or how much you want them to.
- Parents condition our self-beliefs so being a parent is one of the most important roles humans play in life.

I accept that as a little girl, I was an innocent victim of my father's inability to experience meaningful relationships. I do not judge my father or his actions and have forgiven him, as I know that he is on his own personal inner journey.

When I started dating at fifteen, my inner belief system had already been strongly conditioned by my childhood experiences. I subconsciously chose boyfriends based on their ability to fulfil my need for approval and love rather than from a desire for a healthy balanced relationship. Therefore, I attracted boyfriends who may have looked different, but who in essence had uncannily similar characteristics.

My first love lasted two years, and to begin with our relationship was like one from a romantic novel. He was gorgeous looking with blonde hair, blue eyes, a sporty physique and a cheeky smile, as well as being kind, attentive and loving. We had similar interests and so had lots of fun when we were together, spending most weekends at his house so that I could watch him play football and have dinner with his family afterwards. I accompanied him on his French football tour, stopping off at the newly opened Disneyland Paris as well as Monaco, which was magical. When I started sixth form college, however, our relationship changed and he became exceedingly controlling. He didn't want me to go out with my new friends and his attitude changed from attentive to dismissive and his words became aggressive instead of loving. Our relationship ended when he cheated on me with a past school friend. He broke my heart, as I struggled to understand where I had gone wrong in the relationship and why he didn't love me anymore. I also couldn't comprehend why he chose to betray me in favour of simply ending the relationship.

I subconsciously carried this heartbreak and pain into my subsequent relationships. As a therapist, I know the energy cords formed during a relationship, combined with karmic lessons and unhealed wounds, invite in similar relationships through the Law of Attraction. You will read about karma, energy cords and the Law of Attraction in part two of this book, which will provide a clear understanding of how these affect us and the relationships we experience. If I could go back in time, I wonder if I would make the same relationship choices from a healed mindset and sacred heart or make different ones? I do not regret any of my relationships however, as they have shaped me as a human being, taught me so much on a personal level and given me the insight to write this book as well as empathise with others.

When I met Robert, however, I was unaware of the subconscious wounds I carried. I foolishly shared the details of my childhood and relationship issues with him, as I naively thought it best to be open and honest. In reality though, I was providing him with the ammunition he needed to deepen my mental and emotional wounds. I had innocently made myself the ideal target for Robert to use my flaws against me. He knew that I was vulnerable, had little confidence, low self-worth and feared rejection. My wounds kept me locked in victim consciousness and put me in a disabled state where Robert could continuously play out his own personality dysfunctions.

4

History Repeating

In my absolute determination to create a loving and nurturing relationship with Robert, I unintentionally created my worst nightmare. Like my mother before me, I had fallen for a man who was a compulsive liar, a manipulator and a womaniser. History was repeating itself and I was accidentally walking the same path as my mum.

My father is and always will be my father but that doesn't mean that I have to like or approve of his behaviour. He worked hard and played hard; he was a smoker, a drinker and a gambler. On one occasion, he even gambled and lost a week's salary without a thought or care for how he would provide for his family that week. My father's motto was *'always look after number one'* and he lived his life by this mantra. He embarked on multiple affairs during his twenty years of marriage to my mother. Some of these were with the wives of his best friends. The value of loyalty seemed to evade him, as he was incapable of being faithful to his wife, family or friends.

When it suited, my father publically portrayed himself as a dedicated family man. For work purposes, especially at times of promotion, it was important that he showed himself in an idyllic family scene to his bosses. My father would bring his employers home, so that my obedient mother could entertain them with the perfect dinner party. In reality, my father spent little time at home and as a result I have very few positive memories of him.

My father didn't engage much in family life other than special occasions or on our annual family holiday. It was my mother who organised special family events, facilitated them on the day and made them a success. She was the lynch pin that cemented us together, made us feel loved on a daily basis, and created treasured memories. I enthusiastically share my childhood memories with my own children and feel honoured to continue some of my mother's traditions in order to create memories for them.

Whilst growing up, my father's absence from family life was noticeable along with his intolerance of children. I can't remember him ever playing with me, taking me to the park, building sandcastles, playing a board game or having a meaningful conversation. When he was at home, he liked the house free from toys and his views represented the ideology that children should be seen and not heard. If he thought that we were misbehaving or being too noisy, then he would threaten to hit us with a stick that he kept in the garage. The combination of fear mixed with not feeling good enough and my need for approval and acceptance, resulted in my impeccable manners and behaviour as a child.

Sadly, my father was self-centred, selfish and a maverick. He was so self-absorbed and unempathetic towards the thoughts and feelings of others that one Sunday, when I was about 10 years old, he took me with him to meet his 'lady friend'. It didn't seem to matter to him that a little girl would feel confused as to why her father was seeing another lady instead of being at home with his wife; her mother. He seemed to lack the morals and boundaries of a normal, decent human being. Lies were second nature to him.

I didn't want a duplicate of my father as a husband. I had witnessed my father's psychological abuse towards my mother growing up, and the misery she endured. I would discover her crying on more occasions than I care to remember and heard far too many arguments to mention. My father did the following to my mother:

- Put her down using emotional abuse.

- Used isolation to control what she did.

- Limited her friends through seclusion.

- Prevented her from partaking in hobbies.

- Through economic abuse he prevented her from working and restricted her finances by giving her an allowance.

- Used coercion by threatening suicide if she left him.

- Became intimidating with his physical presence.

My father used these strategies so that he held power in the relationship and was the one in control. I didn't want the man I married to replicate my dad as a father for my own sanity, as well as for the wellbeing of my children. I wanted a man who was honest, trustworthy, loving and reliable. I envisaged a man who would partake in family activities, play with his children and engage with them, as well as being a good role model. Unknowingly, when I started dating Robert, I set myself up for disappointment, heartache and psychological abuse.

5

He Loves Me, He Loves Me Not

The first two years of my relationship with Robert were far from stable or consistent. Our roller coaster relationship meant that we dated on and off with unexpected break-ups, which Robert could offer no real reasons for. I moved in with him and then out again on several occasions, adding to my confusion. Robert picked me up and put me down like a play toy. The relationship challenged me emotionally and mentally, causing me immense anxiety and further knocks to my already low self-esteem.

There were numerous signs that the relationship was an unhealthy one, but I didn't seem to recognise them or maybe the fear of confronting them was just far too great. I had my uses however, and Robert would always ask me to accompany him to social events, in order to create the illusion that he was a loyal and committed individual. Those close to him knew what he was truly like though, especially his work colleagues who had worked with him for years and would take numerous personal calls for him from various women.

I remember Robert being invited to the wedding reception of one of his work colleagues, and he asked if I would be his plus one. Of course I was delighted to attend with him and agreed. On the evening of the reception, I was greeted by a colleague of Robert's with the hurtful words, *"Oh he brought you then. We were running a bet at work on who Robert would bring this evening."* Surrounded by happy couples, I immediately felt humiliated and I wanted the ground to swallow me up. I was astonished at the cruelty of the man who greeted me, as well as those who laughed so ignorantly. Did they not realise I was a person with feelings? The women looked at me with embarrassment and sympathy. Predictably, Robert laughed it off as a bad joke, but in my heart I knew his friend's words were true.

Incidents like that were becoming more frequent; I felt like I was going insane. Was my imagination running away with me? Confirmation that I was compos mentis came in the form of news one day from a friend. She informed me that Robert had recently slept with her friend at his house and that she felt I deserved to know the truth. I knew the girl he had slept with, Natasha, as she socialised at the same wine bars that I did. I knew that she was Robert's type; young, tanned, with blonde hair and blue eyes.

I spoke to Natasha and instantly knew that she was telling the truth. She was able to describe Robert's house and bedroom, as well as recall a telephone conversation that I had with Robert whilst she was at his house. The penny finally dropped. I felt physically sick knowing that he had shared his bed with someone else and that I had been intimate with him since then.

I was at the end of my tether and could no longer stand the constant uncertainty and disillusion. I realised that the only person hurting me was me, as I kept allowing Robert to treat me as he did. I knew deep down that I was a good person and deserved to be treated well, with love, respect and dignity. So it was time for me to move on and to do that I had to end the relationship. I told Robert that I didn't want us to date anymore and he didn't seem too bothered. I will go as far to say that he was quite relieved. Even though it was my decision to end the relationship, I was heartbroken, but I kept reminding myself that it was for the best in the long-term.

In order to take my mind off Robert, I arranged a girlie night out with friends on the following Friday. I needed to connect with people who loved me for me and with whom I shared common interests. My friends always enjoyed going out, going to clubs, dancing and having a good time. As usual, we started our night out at the local wine bars, as we knew most people there so had plenty of people to chat to; male and female alike. Great DJs performed there, playing current dance music for us to strut our stuff to. They say time flies when you're having fun and it sure did that evening. The bars were closing up so my friends and I headed to the car park so that we could go to a nightclub. However, when we got back to the car, my mood changed.

My friend, who was sharing a lift with me, noticed a handwritten note secured under my windscreen wiper. It said: '*I have seen you here with a big fat ugly guy and now I see you with an ugly bloke with long hair. You should be with me.*' Did Robert seriously believe that I wouldn't recognise his writing? My friend advised me to ignore the note, as it was another of Robert's mind games, so I put it in my pocket and drove her home, as I was no longer in the mood for clubbing.

After driving my friend home, it was my intention to head home myself, however I was furious. How dare Robert sabotage my first night out with friends and play such tricks with my heart? (In the note, he referred to *himself* as the fat man and the guy with the long hair was my friend.) Unlike Robert I was perfectly capable of having a conversation and a platonic relationship with someone of the opposite sex. He always had an uncanny way of sexualising everything. Foolishly in my anger, I drove to Robert's house to confront him and ask what he was trying to achieve by writing such a note!

The lights were on, so I knew that Robert was already home when I arrived at his house. I knocked on the door and when he opened it I presented him with the note and informed him that I knew it was from him as I recognised his writing. I turned around and headed back to my car, however, as I did so, Robert begged me to talk to him. I hesitated for a moment then continued walking. Robert told me to stop being silly and just talk to him. I stopped, turned around and walked towards his house and told Robert that he had just five minutes to explain, as I wanted to go home.

Robert confessed that seeing me talk to another man that evening had made him jealous. He hated seeing me laughing and joking with someone else and realised that he loved me and wanted to be with me. I reminded Robert that I had given him more than enough chances in the past and that it was obvious that we weren't right for each other. Robert expressed that he felt our relationship was too intense too quickly and it scared him. He felt I was too needy and it was my behaviour which pushed him to fall out with me when he couldn't cope. Although it was my choice to end our relationship on this occasion, it got me thinking; *Maybe he's right, maybe I am too needy!*

Robert begged for forgiveness and explained that it was because he wasn't ready to settle down that he behaved the way he did. He promised that it wouldn't happen again, as he was now ready to commit to our relationship. Natasha had made him realise that I was the one for him, as she meant nothing to him. He explained that she had flirted and pursued him for a long time and that he should never have given in to her.

I felt utterly confused and broke down in tears. I explained to Robert how much he had hurt me and that I couldn't understand what I had done wrong, as I had always done everything he asked of me. I apologised if I was too needy but explained that it was only because I loved him. I still struggled to understand what I had done that was so wrong. I couldn't comprehend how Robert could change his mind so easily or quickly. I wondered if his change of heart was just because he was jealous.

So after talking at length that evening, Robert convinced me to give our relationship another chance and we reunited. Our union improved considerably and he seemed to make much more of an effort, so I was glad that Robert had persuaded me to give our relationship another go. Well, at least I was for a while, or, to be specific, I was until one Sunday morning. when I came downstairs to hear Robert talking on the telephone arranging to meet someone that evening. When I walked into the living room, he quickly concluded the conversation and said, *"I'll see you later then."* I suspected that he wasn't talking to a friend, so I chose to act on my gut response for once.

I politely asked, *"Who was that on the phone, baby?"* whilst walking over to the phone, picking up the receiver and pressing re-dial, to which Robert replied, *"Oh it was just Simon's mother."* I asked Robert why he would be arranging to meet his friend's mother at a wine bar. When Robert saw the receiver in my hand, he screamed, *"What are you doing?"* and grabbed it and proceeded to unplug it from the wall socket. I told him that I didn't believe him and that if he was truly on the phone to Simon's mother, then he would allow me to call her. Robert accused me of being embarrassing and said that he would not allow me to call Simon's mother and ruin their longstanding relationship. I repeated that if he was genuinely talking to her, that he would let me call to put my mind at rest. The argument continued and Robert would not back down, so I felt I had no option but to grab my belongings and leave. Our relationship was finally over, as I could no longer deal with Robert's repeated lies and continuous deceit.

I guess it's true when they say a leopard never changes its spots. I could not cope with the anxiety caused by Robert's continuous fabrications, so I knew that for my own sanity and health it was time to call it a day on our relationship. This time I knew that it was truly over and that Robert would not change my mind. That evening, I went out with my friends as usual to our local wine bars and it was no surprise to see Robert out with his friend and two females. It appeared at first sight to be a double-date and Robert's was a young female with blonde hair and blue eyes. I soon discovered on the grapevine that she was in fact Robert's new girlfriend.

6

Blind Date

With A-Levels complete, I no longer worked at the health club. Instead I had a part-time job at a wine bar three nights per week, whilst studying at the university in the city. It was a great social environment and I had a greater earning potential, due to generous tips kindly gifted by customers. My best friend recommended me to her boss and got me the job there, so working with her was an added bonus.

Out of the blue one day, I received a call from a friend who asked me if I would go out on a blind date with a male friend of hers. Apparently, he had noticed me working at the wine bar one evening and commented to her that he found me attractive. She told him that she knew me and offered to set us up on a blind date. Well for him it wasn't strictly a blind date, but for me it was. I had never been on a blind date before, so I was a little apprehensive, but I successfully put my initial reservations to one side and agreed to go.

The evening of the date soon arrived and I was incredibly nervous. Apart from Robert, I hadn't been on a date for so long that I was concerned I might struggle for things to say and that conversation might dry up. I wasn't looking for a serious relationship, as I had formed the opinion that they were too hurtful and I certainly didn't want to get hurt again. I was also still on the rebound from Robert and was grieving the loss of our relationship. Despite everything Robert had done and all that he had put me through, I still loved him. Mad I know, but true. It was as though I had involuntarily developed Stockholm syndrome. In an unconscious strategy to survive a controlling relationship and intimidation, I had formed a paradoxical emotional bond and positive feelings for my captor. I had disassociated from my own feelings and questioned whether Robert's comments about my behaviour were true. I lived in a constant state of uncertainty, which caused much trauma and stress, triggering the fight, flight or freeze response. My body was awash with physical chemical responses which added to my anxiety. I found it difficult to concentrate, would experience regular nightmares, and experienced feeling of confusion, as well as an increased distrust of others. Robert, on the other hand, viewed himself as my rescuer not my captor, as he would often say to me, "*You know I saved you. I wonder where you would be without me?*"

I knew that I had to move on with my life and put my relationship with Robert behind me, so I decided to make the most of an evening out. Chris was really kind, a good conversationalist and he made me laugh a lot. As first dates go, it was extremely pleasant. At the end of the evening we decided to see each other again, on the understanding that I didn't want to get into another relationship. Chris understood it was too soon after Robert and that I wasn't ready to commit, but I was happy for us to simply enjoy each other's company.

Over the forthcoming weeks, we went on several dates and continued to have fun. He always behaved like the model gentleman and treated me like a princess. Nothing was too much trouble for him but I knew it was unfair to keep seeing him, as his feelings for me had grown and he wanted to be more than just friends. Our time together helped me to realise that I was a good person, attractive and good company. He helped boost my self-confidence which had been at rock bottom when we originally met. Through our encounter, I appreciated that not all men are the same, nor are they all bad. I will always thank him for that.

I decided to focus on my studies, enjoy my part-time job and make the most of my time with friends. I think there's a saying, 'Boyfriends come and go but friends are forever'. Well, it was time to concentrate on my friendships and forget about having a boyfriend for a while. My passion was dance music so my friends and I journeyed to clubs all over the UK, such as *Golden* in Stoke, *The Institute* and *Miss Money Penny's* in Birmingham, as well as *Milwaukee's* in Milton Keynes. We adored going to events such as Cream, Dance Planet and Dreamscape.

Whilst at home one evening, there was a knock at the door. Mother and I weren't expecting anyone, so you can imagine my surprise when she informed me that Robert was at the door. I told her that I didn't want to see or speak to him, which she then reiterated to Robert. He replied that he wouldn't go away until he had spoken to me. I was unwilling for my mother to play piggy in the middle, as she wasn't in the best of health and didn't need any stress. I walked into the hallway and agreed to speak to Robert.

From the doorstep, he asked if he could come in so that we could talk properly but I refused as I did not see the point in a lengthy conversation. He pleaded with me, so to avoid the neighbours knowing my personal business and becoming the local bit of gossip, I stepped to one side and let him in.

Robert explained that he had found out I had been on dates with someone else. I informed him that my private life was just that: private, so none of his business. He said that he regretted us breaking up and that he was missing me immensely. He admitted that he had been dating other women, too, but that when he was with them, he couldn't stop thinking of me. He realised that it was me he wanted and that he had made a terrible mistake.

I told him that it was too late, as he had hurt me on too many occasions, far more than I could forgive him for. I expressed that he made me feel unattractive, useless and worthless and that his repeated rejections were too much to bear. His public put downs had humiliated me on numerous occasions in front of family and friends. I felt as though he wanted a servant to cook, clean and do his laundry rather than someone to experience a balanced, loving relationship with.

I advised Robert that my heart was broken and I didn't feel that it could be mended, nor could I ever trust him again. I communicated to him that I felt like he didn't want me but that he didn't want anyone else to have me either, and reminded him of the car note incident last time he saw me talking to a man. I told him that if he truly loved me, he would let me go, as I deserved to be happy. Robert started crying and confessed that he had made a terrible mistake. He also admitted that he knew it wouldn't be easy if we got back together, however he assured me that he truly loved me but just hadn't fully realised it, until now.

A Tale of Unfortunate Events

R obert and I reestablished our relationship, as I decided to give him another chance. Why? I still loved him and I believed him this time when he said that he had changed and our relationship would be different. We both committed to making it work this time around. We spoke every day on the phone and saw each other on a more regular basis. He was more open about our relationship in public and was extraordinarily attentive. We enjoyed dining in, continued our regular movie nights at the cinema and increased the number of nights out as a couple.

Robert was most definitely making more of an effort with me; his communication improved and he was much more complimentary about my looks, figure and clothes. I also slept over at his house more regularly. As a result, I felt more secure in our relationship, which in turn made me feel more confident in myself. Our relationship was certainly improving, so I was pleased that I had found it in my heart to give Robert another chance. Third time lucky I thought.

Then one morning, we were woken by a loud, consistent banging on the front door. We didn't know who it was or why they were banging the door so ferociously. Robert leapt out of bed, ran downstairs and opened the front door to be confronted by numerous police officers. I could clearly hear the commotion from the bedroom upstairs so I hurried out of bed and hastily got dressed. I wondered what on earth was happening, as it felt as if we were in a movie - as the incident felt so unreal. Some of the officers searched downstairs whilst others immediately came upstairs and started thoughtlessly searching through my overnight bag, which felt extremely degrading.

At this point, we hadn't a clue what they were searching for. The only thing that I considered it could be was Robert's steroids, which he cunningly concealed under a floorboard in the upstairs cupboard. I convinced myself that these were what they were searching for and was petrified that they would find them. Fortunately they were too well concealed and the officer who checked the cupboard didn't notice the loose floorboard.

Time passed slowly and it felt like the officers were searching for ages before they gave up. Thankfully, they didn't find what they were looking for, so their consolidated efforts had been in vain. I assumed they must have made some sort of mistake and that the dreadful ordeal was finally over. One of the officers then turned to Robert and proceeded to read him his rights, charge him with credit card fraud and promptly arrest him. As soon as they arrested him, they frogmarched him out of the house and into a police car, as they were taking him to the police station for questioning. I couldn't comprehend what had happened or what I had heard. Fraud? There must have been a mistake.

After Robert and the police left the house, I was on tenter hooks. I was confused and unsure what to do, as I had no means of speaking to Robert in order to clarify what was happening. Who should I speak to? His friends were all at work and I didn't have their phone numbers anyway, so I made the decision to call Robert's parents, as I knew that if anything happened to me, I would want Robert to call my mother. I spoke to Robert's father and informed him of the morning's events. His father could hear how upset I was, so kindly invited me to go to their house until Robert was released. We sat and waited together, all of us anxious and enormously worried. I drank several cups of tea and watched the clock incessantly, as the combination of not knowing and the feeling of helplessness was extremely stressful.

My mind span around in circles as I considered if Robert could have been involved in any way with credit card fraud. In his professional career, he had no access to money of any description. As well as his full-time job though, Robert also provided security at a designer clothing store at the local shopping centre. Could this be where the fraud had taken place, so therefore the police were simply doing their duty and questioning everyone who worked there?

Robert was finally released and returned back home. I cried with sheer relief when I saw him, as part of me had been scared that the charges were correct and that he might be convicted. Robert clarified that the police were claiming that he and some associates were committing credit card fraud at the local shopping centre. They had released him on bail until his court appearance. To go to court the police must have had evidence, but I couldn't see Robert risking his career for some designer clothes, it just didn't make any sense.

Whilst Robert was explaining what had happened, I saw a vulnerable side to him that I had not seen before. This sixteen stone body builder looked like a small petrified child. He kept telling me how much he loved me and that he needed me more than ever now, as only I could get him through this horrid ordeal. I reassured him that I loved him and that I would help in whatever way I could. Robert then asked me to move back in with him as he needed my full support. Seeing the pain in his eyes, I agreed.

Robert notified his employer of his arrest and that the police had charged him with fraud. He was immediately suspended from work pending an investigation and until further notice. I saw panic in his eyes with the realisation that if found guilty in court, he would lose his job, pension and home, as well serve a prison sentence.

Unable to go to work, Robert soon became depressed and lacked focus, so his best friend offered him work at his health club. This was the ideal solution for Robert, as it gave him a purpose each day, doing something that he loved. However, it was far from ideal for our relationship. My insecurities were resurrected and I became concerned whether Robert could remain faithful. By this time I had left university as I had decided not to return after the first year. I now worked at a local call centre which meant long hours; I worked twelve hour shifts, five days per week, plus a seven hour shift every Saturday.

Whenever I felt insecure I would remind myself of the numerous occasions that Robert told me how much he loved me and that this time he wanted a committed relationship. It was a real challenge to forgive and forget his past actions, but I did my best to draw a line in the sand and start again. He had hurt me so badly though and my heart carried many wounds.

We did our best to maintain a normal life so that we were not consumed by the shadow that hung over us. The constant pressure of the case, however, very rarely left our minds and it was a particularly distressing time. I felt exceedingly sorry for Robert and I worried constantly about the short and long-term damage it may do to him. Robert confided in me that the thought of going to prison and not being with me was breaking his heart. He was hopeful that the charges would be dropped, but in the meantime we had to do our best to continue our life whilst waiting to hear from Robert's solicitor and the courts.

A Much Needed Break

We were invited to attend Robert's friend's wedding in Middlesbrough. I saw this as a wonderful opportunity for him to see his friend get married and socialise with others, as well as a chance to temporarily take our minds off daily anxieties whilst waiting to hear from the courts. A weekend away was what we both desperately needed, as my long working hours didn't allow us to have much quality time together. We organised our wedding outfits, bought a gift and booked a hotel for the night of the wedding. We planned our journey and knew that in order to arrive on time we had to leave at 6.30am on the Saturday morning. This would allow us to check-in to the hotel upon arrival, shower and change our clothes before the wedding itself.

Our best made plans didn't work out, however. Robert didn't want to forfeit his Friday night out with the lads the night before the wedding, so went out as usual. He promised that he wouldn't stay out late, as he understood that we had an early start the next morning. I decided to stay at home in order to prepare for the wedding the next day and enjoyed a pamper evening. I relaxed in an aromatherapy bath, gave myself a facial, waxed my legs and manicured my nails. It was getting quite late by the time I had finished, so I decided to wait up for Robert so that we could go to bed together. I waited and waited but by midnight Robert still wasn't home so I decided to ring his mobile phone to see what time he would be back. To my disappointment, Robert didn't answer his phone, so I left a voicemail and proceeded to bed alone. I didn't settle easily and was restless in bed that evening, watching the clock and sporadically calling Robert's mobile phone to check he was alright. The phone continued to ring out, however, and transferred to his voicemail each time. I began to worry; where could he be? Had he been involved in an accident? Should I call around the hospitals? I was extremely concerned, anxious and scared, as he had promised that he would be home early.

At 6am Robert returned home. I was so relieved that he was home safely but simultaneously angry too, as I couldn't understand why he hadn't taken my calls or called me back to let me know that he was alright. I asked him where he had been but Robert developed amnesia and told me that he couldn't remember. I wish I could blame alcohol for his selective memory, but Robert never drank anything other than soft drinks when he went out. I couldn't comprehend his behaviour or why he was choosing to be so short with me. What had I done? Why was he ruining our plans for a romantic weekend away together after everything we had been through?

Robert got straight into bed, saying that he was tired, he needed to sleep and that we would leave when he was ready. So 6.30am came and went and I paced the house wondering what time we would leave or in fact whether we would miss the wedding altogether. In the end we left home four hours later than planned at 10.30am. The four hour car journey was tense, as Robert was still tired and I was annoyed as it wasn't the relaxed start to the weekend that I had imagined.

We arrived embarrassingly late to the wedding, walking into the church after the ceremony had started. I was highly ashamed, not just for interrupting the ceremony but also because we were underdressed, as we didn't have time to check into the hotel and change our clothes prior to arrival. As a self-conscious person, I also hated making an entrance and much preferred to modestly blend into the background.

The bride looked stunning, the couple looked immensely happy and the ceremony was beautiful. The photographer took some shots at the church and then we all advanced to the hotel for the wedding breakfast. I struggled to relax, as I only knew the bride and her sister who were Robert's friends. The bride had moved from her home town up north a few years earlier, so most of the guests were locals. I did my best to socialise with the other guests, especially those on our table, who were from the bride's home town and therefore local to where we lived. Robert appeared to be the centre of their amusement as they candidly talked about his numerous conquests, which unnerved me. They seemed oblivious to the fact that I may feel hurt by their comments and the details of their recollections.

Their relentless musings triggered my mind to regress to past hurts as well as to the previous night's events. I questioned whether Robert may be up to his old tricks again, as after all he couldn't recollect where he had been or was reluctant to. Robert had kept me in a state of uncertainty before as a means of making me think that I was reading too much into matters or feel like I was crazy. Had I been wrong to give him another chance? Surely he wouldn't persistently chase after me if he didn't love me?

After the wedding breakfast, we went back to our room so that we could finally change our clothes in readiness for the evening reception. I used the opportunity of being secluded from the others to share and discuss my concerns with Robert. He accused me of being paranoid, as he had simply enjoyed a night out with the lads as usual and he couldn't see why there was a problem. I told him how disappointed I was, as I had planned a romantic weekend away to make up for the lack of quality time we had together when at home. I questioned why he couldn't remember where he had been and he responded that it shouldn't matter where he was, as all I needed to know was that he was just out with the lads. I then enquired why he didn't come back as promised, as he knew that we had an early start the next day, but he simply stated that he lost track of time and that I was acting as if I didn't trust him. The truth was that I really didn't trust him; how could I?

Robert used his charm and charisma to swiftly divert the focus of our conversation. He used intimacy as a means of resolving conflicts, personal gratification and further mind control. By being submissive to his sexual needs, I would please Robert, obtain his approval and feel loved by him. My weak sexual boundaries, however, resulted in me participating when I didn't want to, in order for me to get the acceptance I craved. Robert effectively avoided our issues again and successfully brushed the previous night's incident under the carpet.

To Be Or Not To Be

As we hoped, Robert's case was thrown out of court due to the statements of key witnesses being discredited. Thankfully the Crown Prosecution Service dropped all charges which meant that we could now let go of the stresses of the past few months and resume ordinary life. Robert's suspension was lifted, so he no longer had to work at the health club and returned to his full-time job. I was secretly pleased that he would be spending less time at the gym, as his time there unquestionably put a strain on our relationship.

To celebrate his absolution we decided to book a two week holiday in order to put the past behind us and start afresh. The holiday would coincide with my forthcoming twenty-first birthday so we had much to celebrate. It was the first holiday that we'd had together as a couple so I felt this was a huge step forward in our relationship, as before Robert had only ever wanted to go on holiday with his friends.

We would finally get to spend some quality time together and I prayed that our holiday would be an improvement on our romantic weekend away in Middlesbrough. I was also looking forward to laying on a beach in a sunny climate, relaxing and having fun, just the two of us with no distractions. A holiday was what we both needed and deserved after such a chaotic and stressful year. I intended to make the most of our time together and create a holiday to remember.

We got off the airplane and were greeted by the blistering Caribbean sunshine. We collected our luggage and then transferred from the airport to the hotel by coach. We were both really pleased with our choice of hotel as it and the grounds were beautiful. We checked in at reception to rapidly learn that our accommodation was a twin room instead of a double. I was mortified, as twin beds didn't exactly provide the most appropriate ambience for a romantic holiday. Robert told the receptionist that twin beds were fine and explained that it gets really hot at night in the Caribbean so it was probably for the best that we had separate beds. I wasn't going to let this small set back ruin our holiday. I should have realised that twin beds were a bad omen and a universal sign of things to come.

It wasn't quite the exclusive couple's holiday I had imagined because our friends came along too. It was lovely, however, to have the ability to chill out on the beach all day with no timetable to adhere to like at home. We were staying at an all-inclusive hotel, so it was fabulous to eat such an extensive range of food at any time of day. Robert certainly took advantage of the all-day eating experience and for once I wasn't concerned about my weight and ate what I wanted. The freedom of the experience was liberating.

I was looking forward to fully embracing the Caribbean night life but sadly Robert had no interest in staying up late and wanted to go to bed early most evenings. Our wants and needs for the holiday were not in alignment but poles apart. Although disappointed, I respected the fact that Robert needed to rest after the terrible ordeal he had experienced. He needed time to switch off and recharge his batteries.

During the first week of the holiday, it became apparent how volatile our relationship was when we had an argument whilst playing chess by the pool. It was a stupid quarrel that was blown out of all proportion, but it was enough to make Robert completely ignore me for three days. I was incredibly lonely over that period and Robert used isolation as a means of control and cut communication to highlight his power. He spent all of his time with our friends to limit my involvement and segregate me further.

I desperately wanted to go home and enquired with the travel representative about boarding an earlier flight, but I didn't have enough money. Robert happily witnessed me dining, sitting on the beach and attending the evening entertainment alone, but it didn't seem to bother him in the slightest. The uncomfortable silence when we were in the room together was insufferable so I apologised to Robert in order to dissolve the conflict. Robert blamed my actions for the disagreement and belittled me by saying that I had been silly. I wanted to bring an end to the tiff so chose to suppress my true thoughts and feelings so that we could enjoy the remainder of the holiday.

The following week, Robert arranged for the two of us to go on a day trip to the island's capital. It was a welcome change to the restrictions of the hotel complex and it meant that we would also get exclusive time together, away from our friends. The bus journey there was enlightening, as the Caribbean homes and way of life were in stark contrast to the hotel complex. We walked around the town, visited the tourist shops and ate lunch before walking along the harbour.

Out of the blue, Robert ushered me into a jewellery store and instructed me to choose a ring. I enquired why and he smiled and said that he wanted to buy me an eternity ring as a birthday gift. I was ecstatic, yet at the same time confused, as his behaviour was so changeable. I was becoming accustomed to our relationship's high and lows and began to wonder if all relationships were like this behind closed doors. After all, *he wouldn't buy me a ring if he didn't truly love me, would he?* We spent a while in the shop talking to the assistant and finally selected a beautiful ruby eternity ring which looked beautiful on my lefthand ring finger. It was the perfect end to a perfect day.

We both embraced what was left of the holiday and made the most of the little time we had left. Robert was more attentive; he took me on my first jet ski ride, stayed up later at night and looked after me when I was ill. The exotic food wasn't agreeing with me and I awoke each morning feeling nauseous. I decided to stick to very plain food for the remainder of the holiday and avoid alcohol, as the mere smell of it made me feel sick. Even on the last evening, which was my 21st birthday, I couldn't stomach a celebratory drink.

We packed our things and said our goodbyes to the Caribbean. It had been a memorable holiday in many ways, both good and bad. Our roller coaster vacation reflected our relationship, with its fantastic highs but miserable lows. Disappointingly though, it was never the romantic encounter that I had initially imagined. Our return flight was miserable as we got caught in the tail winds of a hurricane. I was overjoyed when we finally landed and couldn't wait to get back home.

When we finally got home, Robert went into town to get some medication for my sickness. He returned with a pregnancy testing kit that he had purchased from the chemist. I laughed when I opened the bag and told him that it would be impossible for me to be pregnant whilst taking the contraceptive pill. Robert believed that my holiday sickness was actually morning sickness, so he asked me to do the test. I went into the bathroom, did the test and waited nervously.

The test confirmed that we were going to have a baby. Robert was overjoyed and voiced that all he ever wanted was to be a father. Our relationship was still so turbulent and unpredictable, however, and although Robert was twenty nine years old, I wasn't sure that he was ready to have a family of his own. His convincing words told a story of commitment but his actions were ambiguous. I was in complete shock. I loved children and wanted to be a mother, but I never imagined starting a family so young. I didn't want an abortion though, as I could never willingly take the life of another human being. A termination was NOT an option, therefore my path was mapped out for me.

10

Great Expectations

Robert was so excited at the prospect of being a father and couldn't wait to share our news with his family and friends. His mother and father, although already grandparents, were over the moon that their youngest and favourite son was starting a family. My mother was astounded with our news when we initially informed her, but also exceedingly pleased to be expecting her first grandchild.

I imagined our pregnancy as a magical experience for us both to share and envisaged the forthcoming months being filled with quality time together, love, affection and support. I expected the pregnancy to be the turning point in our relationship and believed that we could put our past differences behind us once and for all. I prayed that we would now be united in order to make our relationship and family a success and achieve a fairy tale 'happy ever after'.

I had high hopes for our pregnancy and I was committed to doing the very best I could for myself and our unborn child. My intention was to eat healthily, continue to exercise and to educate myself as much as possible regarding the pregnancy, birth and raising a child. I very much wanted to be the best mum in the world to our little girl or boy, and make Robert and my family tremendously proud.

Continuing to work long shifts, six days per week, was challenging and draining, so the pregnancy took its toll on my body. On weekdays I returned home at 8.30pm to cook and eat dinner, have a bath and then go to bed. I was incapable of doing anything else as I was so utterly exhausted. With a baby on the way, however, I had to continue working long shifts in order to buy what we needed for the baby. Robert's wage wasn't much back then in 1996 as he was on the basic grade and he rarely had the opportunity to do any overtime. So, it was my responsibility to earn extra reserves.

In addition to work, the horrendous morning sickness, which lasted until late afternoon, also took its toll on me physically. I ate ginger biscuits first thing in the morning as suggested, to alleviate the sickness, but there was no improvement. Upon arrival at work, the smell of coffee made me gag and at home, the sight of raw chicken and the smell of cooking pasta made me want to vomit. I had no control over what was happening to my body and it was as if my body controlled me. I craved king-size Mars bars at all times of the day, Indian curries, chicken pie and chips with lots of vinegar and copious portions of pizza as well as having a permanent thirst for jersey milk. Junk food was fast becoming my staple diet, which wasn't what I had initially planned for me and the baby. The combination of calorific food, along with my inability to exercise, resulted in speedy weight gain.

Coping with the sickness whilst at work was unpleasant and embarrassing. Working in a large call centre, I didn't get any privacy as the desk arrangement was open plan. One day I put a customer on hold without explanation, as during our conversation nausea washed over me. I ran to the toilet to throw up and left her on hold for a considerable amount of time. When I returned to my desk I expected her to have hung up but instead she expressed how infuriated and dissatisfied she was with me. I explained that I was pregnant and apologised profusely, to astonishingly receive an apology in return along with her congratulations. I was relieved, as my emotions were on a hair trigger. I was crying at the slightest upset and didn't want to go through a disciplinary at work. It was a sickening time in more ways than one.

Whilst I adapted and changed in readiness for parenthood, Robert's life didn't actually alter. He still went to the gym every day, went out with the lads each week and pretty much did what he wanted, when he wanted. His excuse was that when our baby was born, he would no longer be able to do those things. He had a point and I wanted to believe him as I loved him dearly, but I had a niggling doubt, which highlighted to me that I still didn't trust him. I wondered how I had ended up pregnant and having a baby with a man I didn't trust. I told myself to stop focusing on Robert's past mistakes and reminded myself that he was different now. If he didn't want to be with me, he simply wouldn't, as he could happily continue his life without me. Robert had expressed on numerous occasions that he was ready to settle down and start a family. He wouldn't lie about something as important as a child.

Sadly, my levels of worry and anxiety never subsided during the pregnancy and remained high throughout. I needed reassurance, love and support from Robert but it came infrequently and only when he was willing to offer it to me on his terms. When his words were forthcoming, his reassurance was mixed with invalidating comments, leaving me in a state of confusion and adding to my perplexed state. I excused Robert's behaviour and tried to believe that it was habitual but my heart wondered if he was consciously saying and doing these things as a means of power and control.

Whilst enjoying a quiet, relaxing day at home one day, the phone rang. When I answered it, I was greeted by the voice of one of the female instructors from the gym. She was polite on the phone and informed me that the receptionist had locked herself in the toilet and wouldn't come out until she had spoken to Robert. I couldn't believe what I was hearing. You see, Robert and the receptionist were rumoured to have dated whilst we were on a break. Why had she locked herself in the toilet? And why would she only come out for him? I found the actions of the instructor cruel and unsympathetic, as who in their right mind would call a pregnant woman and ask the father of her child to go to the gym to speak to his alleged ex? The phone call was bizarre.

Robert took the phone from me and spoke to the instructor, informing her that he would be there in ten minutes. We lived close to the health club, so Robert walked there from our house. After he had hung up the phone, he reassured me that the receptionist was being silly and that he would be back as soon as he could. I stupidly assumed Robert would be back in half an hour but I waited at home for over two hours. When he finally walked through the door, he gave no apology or explanation, other than she was having boyfriend trouble. I asked Robert if she could have talked about the boyfriend trouble with the instructor who had called, or one of her friends, but Robert ignored my question and brushed it under the carpet, like always.

In my head, the gym had become a negative place, which caused massive concern for me every time he went, as it seemed always shrouded in secrecy and deceit. Robert rang one evening from his mobile and said that he would be late home, as he was helping the co-owner with something. I told him that I would wait for him so that we could have dinner together. As soon as I hung up the phone, my mind went into overdrive, my body into panic and my gut instinct suspected something was going on. I reminded myself of the occasion when I had listened to my gut instinct and it was right, so I let go of my fears and acted on my intuition. I picked up the phone and called the co-owner, who was a customer in my father's pub as well as my past employer whilst at college. As suspected, he confirmed that Robert wasn't with him, so I decided to walk to the gym.

Upon arrival, Robert was stood next to the running machine chatting to a lady who was no more than nineteen years old. I couldn't believe my eyes, I felt instantly sick and my legs turned to jelly. I thought I was going to collapse but somehow I found the strength to remain on my feet and call out his name. He turned around and it was very clear from the look on his face that he wasn't expecting to see me. In that instant, his face spoke a thousand words. Incredibly upset, I walked immediately out of the gym and went home.

I was utterly distraught whilst walking home and retreated into my own little world. I caught the attention of passers-by with my loud, uncontrollable sobs but I didn't care. My mind raced with so many questions. I asked myself:

- What have I done wrong?
- Am I unattractive and he wants someone prettier?
- Am I not good enough?
- Does he find me boring?

I then questioned:

- Why does Robert continue to lie to me?
- Does he truly love me?
- Why is he so cruel to me if he loves me?
- Can I ever trust him?
- Why would he say that he couldn't have chosen a better person to have children with, if he can't be faithful to me?

Robert was slowly destroying me. I felt a failure; vulnerable, weak and pathetic. How could someone I loved and who was meant to love me too, cause me so much anguish? I felt absolutely heartbroken and confused. I loved him so much and wanted to trust him, after all, I was about to have his child. I reminded myself that on some level Robert did love me, and that above all he loved children. He had demonstrated this with his young niece and nephew when we took them out on day trips. Maybe once he saw our child, he would put us first. Perhaps Robert just needed his last few months of freedom. Maybe it is possible for a leopard to change its spots.

I couldn't think clearly and feared making a decision in case it was the wrong one. It was clear, however, that I only had two options; I could either leave and bring up our child alone or accept that our relationship would never run smoothly and buckle up for a roller coaster ride. My deepest fears had been realised, I had settled for a man like my father; a liar and a cheat. I could never understand why my mother had tolerated my father's behaviour, especially for so many years, but now I understood why. She loved him, as I loved Robert. My mother was a strong woman to have lived her life in that way, but I wasn't sure I could be that strong.

Maybe long-term it was best to separate now, so I confronted the many uncertainties and questions that were spinning in my head. I considered:

- Where would we live?

- How would I manage as a single mum?

- How would I juggle work and childcare?

- How would I financially support myself and my child?

It broke my heart to think about our future and the possibility of our child growing up in two homes, but I reasoned that it would be all he/she had experienced since birth. I also had to be a realist and consider how I would feel only seeing my child part-time.

The possibility of our child being raised in two separate homes was too much to bear, as I wanted to be a full-time mum. So my only option was to put up and shut up, just like my mother had done in her marriage. The universe had given me the opportunity to leave Robert on numerous occasions, and I was the one who had chosen to forgive him and stay in our relationship. I had no one to blame but myself, so now I had to lie in the bed that I had created.

I lost a part of me that day; a soul fragment disappeared into the ether. My heart struggled to cope with the perpetual emotional abuse and my mind with the ceaseless mental cruelty. With every deceit, forgiving Robert had become increasingly difficult, so in order to cope I compartmentalised my pain and locked it away in a box.

Despite the emotional traumas, physical exhaustion, continuous sickness and a diabetes scare, I loved being pregnant. Every day I woke up feeling very blessed that I had the opportunity to nurture a child, not just whilst pregnant, but for the rest of my life. I felt a deep connection to my unborn child, maybe because we both started life as an accident. Although our child wasn't planned, he/she was most definitely wanted and I vowed that he/she would grow up knowing that, as well as feeling exceptionally loved.

I made the most of the nine months I had by creating a special bond between myself and our child. I regularly talked and sang to the little person that was growing so quickly inside me and couldn't wait for us to meet. I may have been only twenty one, but I knew that I would love and care for our child no matter what, and that I would be the best mother I could be.

11

A Miracle is Born

We welcomed our little miracle, Freya Evans, into the world one cold Sunday morning in 1997. She was perfect in every way, truly beautiful and exceedingly angelic, with piercing blue eyes. As soon as I saw her my heart melted and I was overcome with unconditional love. I held her carefully in my arms, looked into her eyes and knew that I was the luckiest person alive.

The labour lasted just over fourteen hours, but I can honestly say that it was worth every minute. People claim that once you hold your newborn child, the memory of pain disappears and they are right. All I could feel was overwhelming love and joy as I cradled her. It saddened me deeply that Robert had not been with me for the whole experience, as I felt that it would have provided us with time to bond on a new level. However, when I went into labour on the Saturday evening, Robert was working a night-shift.

The previous evening, Robert had briefly returned home at approximately 10pm, to get a change of clothes following an incident at work. I was already having contractions when he arrived and felt ready to go into hospital. Robert thought it best for him to go back to work, as we were unsure how long I was going to be in labour. He suggested that my mother should take me to hospital and to call him when I was close to delivery. My mother and I did as instructed; we grabbed my overnight bag and drove to the maternity hospital.

I had a reality check when we arrived, after seeing the equipment and hearing the noises of other mothers in labour. I was about to give birth to child; a human being who would be dependent on me for much more than just love. I prayed that I would be good enough, that I would be the mother he/she deserved. I also hoped that my child would love me as much as I already loved it.

Throughout the pregnancy, I did my best to avoid birth horror stories, as I wanted the birth to be a positive experience for us all. I didn't want either of us to be pumped full of chemicals, so I requested that the birth be as natural as possible. The pain soon became too much, so the midwife suggested I tried gas and air to help ease the discomfort from the contractions. It made me feel really light-headed and nauseous, so the midwife took it from me and suggested that I have a pethidine injection instead. I reminded her that I wanted a natural birth and that I was adamant I didn't want any drugs. Seeing my agony, the midwife sympathetically suggested that I take a warm bath to ease the discomfort I was experiencing.

Bathing in warm water helped me to relax, but didn't help the pain and I became increasingly restless. I was like a yo-yo, in and out of the bath every half an hour or so as I couldn't decide what I wanted. One minute I wanted to soak in the warm water but the next I couldn't stand the water on my skin and was too hot. I wanted to walk around and then the next moment I wanted to lie down. I couldn't properly decide what I wanted, as my needs were so changeable.

My mother was truly amazing; so patient, kind and considerate. She gently massaged my stomach and back to help with the pain and constantly reassured me how well I was doing. She was unbelievably calm on the surface, although she later confessed how worried she was and how helpless she felt. She hid her concerns well, however, and was my physical and emotional rock throughout; I couldn't have coped without her.

My contractions got worse and closer together but my waters still hadn't broken. The nurses were concerned and asked for my permission to break them, but I was scared and I didn't want them to in case Robert missed the birth of our child. My mother telephoned Robert and asked him to come to the hospital immediately.

When Robert arrived, I was taking another bath, but by now I was delirious with pain. Initially, Robert found this amusing, but he soon became concerned when I continued to slur my words and talk utter nonsense. The midwife and my mother suggested to Robert that I have a shot of pethidine, as it would provide me with pain relief I needed and help calm the baby - the heart monitor had shown that she was in distress. Robert agreed and I received a shot of pethidine, although I have no recollection of this.

The pain subsided and I was able to take a much needed nap to recharge my batteries. As a result, our baby's heart beat also stabilised. When I awoke, I felt more relaxed, had considerably more energy and stopped worrying so much. My waters broke and it was time to deliver our baby.

I was so pleased when Freya was born, but my happiness soon turned to trepidation, when the doctor and midwives took her away in order to clear her nasal passages and throat with tubes. I anxiously waited to hear her cry and when she did I felt incredible relief. Freya was handed to me and I fell instantly in love. I rested her gently on my chest and enjoyed being lost in the moment.

Within 20 minutes of giving birth, I was informed that a newspaper photographer was waiting outside to take our photograph. I was confused until Robert explained that the local rag wanted to feature a story about the birth of his daughter and the previous night's incident at work. I was not in the mood to pose for a photo as I was worn out and I wasn't appropriately dressed. The midwife dressed me in a green hospital robe whilst my mother combed my hair, in an attempt to make me look half decent. The photographer came in, took a few shots and then left.

After the initial emotional high, exhaustion set in so I ate a sandwich and then gave Freya her first feed. When finished, I was asked by one of the midwives if we could move out of the delivery room onto the ward, but I felt reluctant to do so. I just wanted to be on my own with Freya and Robert. The midwife insisted and brought a wheelchair into the room so that Robert could transfer me onto the ward.

When we arrived on the ward, I was pleased to discover that we had a bed by the window so that I could see daylight and connect with the outside world, even if it was through a pane of glass. We settled into our new temporary home quickly and Robert decided it was time for him to leave so that I could rest. It was also time for him to meet his friends at the pub for the traditional act of wetting the baby's head. Mum decided it was also time for her to leave, to catch up on some much needed sleep as she was shattered.

Once on my own, I realised that hospitals can be very impersonal and lonely places. There may have been lots of people around but the nurses were all busy and the new mums were so exhausted that most were asleep. I felt very alone and unsure what was expected of me. I stared in wonder at the little bundle of joy that lay next to me in her cot. As I did so, I felt my heart expand in my chest with the enormity of the love I had for her. The range of emotions I experienced are completely inexpressible in words alone; she was my tiny miracle and a huge blessing. I whispered to her that I would always love her, care for her, support her and accept her for who she was. I promised her that I would cherish my role as her mother and that I felt honoured to be part of her life.

I made the most of my time resting in hospital between visiting hours and Freya's feeds. The few days I had there gave me important bonding time with Freya, as well as the time I needed to reflect on my past and contemplate my future. I prayed that when we both went home, life would be happy for both of us. I sincerely wanted Freya to have the best possible start in life and to experience a stable and loving home.

12

Bitter Sweet Symphony

Freya and I were allowed home two days after her birth. Incredibly that day, we woke up to snow fall which was an unexpected but a very pleasant surprise. After breakfast, I got myself washed and dressed and then enjoyed getting Freya ready in the fabulous new outfit we had previously bought in preparation for her arrival. I felt incredibly excited about taking her home.

My mother had prepared our house meticulously well for our home coming; she had stocked up the fridge, warmed the house and had positioned Freya's crib in the living room. When I stepped through the front door I felt overwhelming relief and instantly relaxed in familiar surroundings. I was liberated from the confines and routines of the hospital and could experience the freedom and independence of doing what I wanted, when I wanted.

The peace and quiet didn't last long, as we experienced a continuous flow of visitors for a few hours that day and during the weeks that followed. In total, we received over 60 new baby cards and an abundance of kind gifts. Everyone was so generous and our friends couldn't wait to meet Freya. Who could blame them, as she was adorable.

Robert played the proud father role extremely well and was very hands on. We clearly defined our new roles; I was on feeding duty whilst Robert was responsible for nappy changes. Robert's shift pattern allowed us to spend lots of time together as a family, especially as I was on 12 weeks maternity leave from work. We enjoyed a glorious summer that year and it was a pleasure to spend time together as a family unit. It was clear to see that Robert loved his daughter and seeing them together warmed my heart. I believed that it was the beginning of a new chapter; one of hope, love and happiness.

August bank holiday was approaching and I had plans for us to spend it together as a family. My dreams were soon shattered, however, when Robert came home one evening and informed me that he was going to Cornwall with friends. I couldn't believe what I was hearing, as I knew the town that they were planning to go to was known for its drunken shag fests. I struggled to understand why he wanted to go to a destination for singletons when we had a four month old daughter.

Robert had made his decision and didn't want a discussion, leaving me in a place of uncertainty once more. Showing concern, he simply stated in a soft voice, *"Don't you trust me?"* I was in a double bind, as if I said I trusted him, he would say, *"What's the problem with me going then?"* and if I said I didn't trust him, he would say, *"Well why are you with me then?"* I felt guilty for not trusting him, as we had a child together, but the truth was that I still didn't trust him. He had promised that once we had a child, there would be no more holidays with the lads and yet here he was going away with his friends again. His strategy to make me feel guilty worked and I felt pressured to condone his trip.

Robert went to Cornwall as planned with his friends. I felt positively sick when he kissed me goodbye and got into his friend's car. In my state of uncertainty, my imagination began to work overtime, causing my anxiety levels to go through the roof. I knew however, that there was nothing that I could do, as Robert would behave in whatever manner he chose. I also knew that his friends had a promise of *'what happens on tour, stays on tour'*, so if Robert did do anything, I would never get to find out.

Rather than stay at home alone, I called the girlfriend of one of Robert's friends to invite her over for a girlie night in with a takeaway, bottle of wine and a movie. She thanked me for the invitation but informed me that she already had plans to go out with her boyfriend. I was surprised to discover that her boyfriend hadn't gone to Cornwall and then I continued to learn that neither had the other lads in the group. She told me that the only two who had gone away was Robert and Stuart, his single friend. I politely wished her a lovely evening and hung up the telephone. I felt positively sick to my stomach and my heart ached. Why had Robert lied about who was going away with him?

I woke the next morning exhausted, as I'd had very little sleep. I did my best to occupy my time but my mind wouldn't stop worrying. Robert called home to see how Freya and myself were and to tell me that he was missing us. He said that he was finding Cornwall boring already and he wanted to come home. I called his bluff and said, *"Come home then"*, but Robert said that he wouldn't be able to get back, as they were car sharing. I enquired who he was sharing a room with and the lies continued to flow freely from his lips as he replied, *"Stuart and Ben"*. I couldn't take his blatant lies anymore, so I confronted him and stated that I knew he was in Cornwall with just Stuart.

The phone went quiet for a while and then Robert informed me that the others had planned to go but they had all dropped out at the last minute. Of course, I knew that he was telling more lies, but I hadn't the energy to argue, as I was far too angry and upset. Robert swiftly changed the subject but I just wanted to get off the phone, as the sound of his voice was going straight through me, like nails down a blackboard. In order to finish the conversation, I told him to have a good time and I would see him when he got back. I put down the telephone and broke into tears, as this supposedly new chapter was just a repeat of those which had gone before. My life was going around in ever decreasing circles with patterns of happiness, tension, some type of incident and then a reunion. That weekend was another incident in a long line of many, and so it became a bank holiday to remember, but for all the wrong reasons.

Robert returned home on bank holiday Monday and walked through the front door as if nothing had happened. He kissed me on the cheek and asked how Freya had been, whilst picking her up from her crib to give her a hug. He was attempting to brush matters under the carpet again. I loved him so much but struggled to look at him, as anger bubbled under the surface of my calm exterior. I smiled subserviently to cover my hurt and hold back my tears. I now truly understood what was meant by a love-hate relationship. I loved the side of Robert that could be loving and caring and hated the side of him that was deceitful and selfish. Robert was a Jekyll and Hyde character. However, unlike Jekyll, Robert had no desire to destroy his darker side. Robert seemed happy living with a dual personality.

Robert unpacked his clothes and put them in the washing basket. The following day, whilst Robert was out of the house, my instincts guided me to check his clothes before I washed them. Part of me wanted to dismiss my feelings through fear of what I may find, but another part of me wanted to honour them, as I deserved to know the truth. I grabbed his clothes from the basket and immediately noticed that one of his shirts reeked of ladies perfume and another had make-up around the collar. Upon his return home later that day, I questioned Robert about Cornwall and begged him to be honest with me about what had really happened on his weekend away.

He was like a parrot repeating word for word the same statement, as if it were a memorised script. *"I just wanted a few days away with my mate Stuart."* I sucked in my anger and frustration, as I knew that by continuing the conversation Robert would just get mad. What was the point in wasting my time and breathe, as Robert was a compulsive liar and incapable of telling the truth? So I joined Robert and buried my head in the sand. *'If you can't beat them join them'*, isn't that what people say?

13

A New Horizon

I returned to work following my maternity leave and adapted to my new life, which consisted of juggling a baby, a house and part-time work. Meanwhile, Robert worked, went to the gym and went out with his friends. I don't question that Robert loved Freya and I suppose me as well, in his own way, but I think that he struggled to control the side of him which needed female attention to boost his ego.

Not long after Freya's first birthday, Robert announced that he wanted us to move house. I was surprised that he wanted to vacate his former bachelor pad and beloved property, which was registered solely in his name. Maybe this proclamation was a positive step towards creating a better life together. We found the perfect renovation project only a few miles from where we lived, so we put in an acceptable offer. Although the house was in a bad state of repair, Robert and I could see its potential and we adored its original features, such as the tiled hallway, high ceilings and open fireplaces. Our only issue was that it was un-inhabitable until certain works were completed, as the old lead pipes, for example, made the water undrinkable and the lack of gas to the property meant that we had no means of heating the house sufficiently. We weren't worried though, as we soon found a solution.

Whilst the building works were being carried out, Freya and I moved into my mother's two bed apartment and Robert moved into his parents' three bed house. This arrangement was temporary and only until we had built the extension, had gas installed in the house, central heating fitted, the metal windows replaced with double glazing and the essential rooms decorated.

Money was tight, so we had to do much of the work ourselves or get friends and family to help when they could. Robert spent his days off work at the house and I helped when I could get childcare for Freya. The house consumed time and money and we completely underestimated how much of both the house would take. Progress was slow and our family home seemed to be slipping further away, just like our relationship. We spent very little family time together other than evening meals, and the growing financial pressures caused regular arguments.

Financial reprieve came in the form of a promotion at work. I may have felt a failure as a girlfriend, but work was an area that I succeeded in. I was an honest and thorough employee and I was flattered when this was recognised. I was headhunted by the business department within the company I worked for, and although I hadn't given any thought about leaving my current role, I felt ready for a new challenge. I had been promoted as far as I could go in the department I worked in, unless I was willing to work full-time again on a twelve hour shift rota. This was fine before I had Freya but was now impractical with Robert's shifts and a young child to care for.

So I gladly accepted my new role within the company. My hours increased and I was working full-time again, but at least my hours were static from 9am until 5.30pm and weekdays only. When I accepted the role, I was excited at my new prospects but also nervous as I didn't fully understand what was expected of me and what the role entailed.

Everyone in the department was so lovely to me and helpful when I arrived. I settled in quickly as I was a fast learner and soon became knowledgeable with regards to my role and new responsibilities. My transition was made easier by the fact that the new department supervisor had worked with me before. Having a familiar face around helped me to settle in and like me, she also had to learn the ropes, so was empathetic.

After six months in my new position, I felt confident in my role and enjoyed going into work each day. I knew that I had embraced the challenge to learn new systems, information and procedures, and had built strong relationships with my colleagues and customers. I had gone above and beyond my duty, putting in massive amounts of time, effort and commitment. I stupidly thought that this would be appreciated and recognised. However, my supervisor had a change of persona and her attitude towards me altered. I couldn't understand what I had done that riled her so much, but she seemed insistent on giving me a hard time. This uncertainty caused my confidence to fall and her frequent invalidating comments in front of my colleagues humiliated me.

My mother was my confidante and best friend, and so I shared my upset with her. As a mother it's difficult to see your child hurting, no matter how old they are, but my mother knew that my current dilemma would provide me with an opportunity to learn and grow as an individual. She bought me a gift to help me; it was a book entitled 'Nasty People' by Jay Carter. I began reading that evening and was instantly captivated by the author's easy to read style and compelling contents. I couldn't put the book down, as it made complete and utter sense to me. I gained valuable insights into why my supervisor behaved the way she did and understanding about some of Robert's behaviour too. A light bulb had been switched on in my head; I was being invalidated by other people and allowing myself to be a victim.

I was a victim in my relationship with Robert, and had allowed myself to be, as well as in my relationship with my father and supervisor. It was as if I was compelled to be a victim; to do what was demanded of me, but all I had to show for it was misery. I lived my life under constant stress and whilst I thought I was handling it, I simply wasn't. I was allowing Robert's invalidating personality to continually control me in order to fulfil his desire for power.

My relationship with Robert had hit an all-time low. Living apart was taking its toll, which was never concrete in the first place. There was a real disconnect between the two of us as we never spent any time together and when we did, it was like we had nothing in common anymore, other than Freya of course. Robert would visit a few nights per week to see Freya, but that was it. I was living life as a single mum, working full-time and bringing Freya up on my own, with the assistance of my mother who was an amazing help and support - emotionally and physically. My personal life was falling apart and I didn't know how to rescue it.

I existed from one day to the next with little joy in my life other than Freya and my mother. Each day for work, I would put on my make-up mask and dress in a suit to hide what I was really thinking and feeling. My mask didn't fool everyone though, as Robert was well-known by many of my work colleagues and they knew the truth about him. One colleague in particular, Edward, was well versed on Robert's behaviour and could see clearly through his public family man act. He was also capable of seeing through mine too, and so asked me one day why I stayed with Robert. I surprised myself and instead of saying, *"Because I love him"*, I found myself saying, *"Because I've made my bed, so I have to lie in it and anyway, who would want to be with a single mum or take on another man's child?"* It was a rhetorical question and yet Edward answered, *"I would."*

Edward and I had much in common and had similar personalities, but we were work colleagues and nothing more. Our relationship was a platonic one and that was how I wanted it to remain, although it was evident that Edward had other desires. Edward wasn't the type of person to say such things in jest, so I was flattered, but I also didn't understand what he found attractive about me, as I was an emotional wreck.

I wanted Robert to want me as Edward did, but the fact was he didn't and I couldn't force him to. He loved me in his own way but not in the way I needed to be loved. I knew in my heart that Robert and I couldn't continue as we were, as it was destructive for all concerned, especially Freya, who was growing up quickly.

I plucked up the courage to tell Robert that it was time for us to sell the house and go our separate ways. Robert never took kindly to being told what to do, after all it meant that he had lost his power and was no longer in control. He accused me of being stupid and that I was reacting to the stress of the house, financial pressures and living apart. I went into a state of self-doubt and questioned whether I was maybe exhausted and overreacting. Robert then turned on his charm and persuaded me that once we moved into the house, we would be a proper family. He said, *"We both love each other, so surely we should stay together for Freya's sake, we owe it to her, don't we?"*

14
New Home, New Start

Robert wanted us to be a family, so we committed our time and effort into getting the house into a liveable state. We knew that we couldn't get the renovation project finished in its entirety, as we simply didn't have the funds. We prioritised what work needed to be done to make the house habitable and then proceeded to decorate Freya's bedroom, our bedroom and the living room. We also ensured that the kitchen and bathroom were both fitted out too.

On the day we moved into the house I experienced mixed emotions. I was sad to be leaving my mother and apprehensive about moving back in with Robert. Freya seemed really happy though, and loved her new bedroom, along with her new moving in present; a black and white lop eared rabbit called Patch. We settled into the house much quicker than I anticipated and we soon became reacquainted as a family once more.

Three months after moving into our new family home, Robert and I decided that we all deserved a family holiday; in fact, it would be our first holiday together as a family. We contemplated where to go for a while until our friends suggested accompanying them to the south of France. Robert and I arranged time off work, booked the flights and hotel and informed Freya of our plans. Freya had never been on a plane, so she was incredibly excited and frequently talked about her forthcoming holiday with family and friends. She also enjoyed going to the shops to buy her holiday clothes and packing her suitcase was a whole new experience for her.

When the day arrived Freya, could no longer contain her excitement. From the moment she got up, to when we arrived at the airport, she displayed a huge grin on her face. When we boarded the plane, we decided it was best to sit Freya in the middle of Robert and I. As always, she behaved impeccably and saw the flight as an adventure. During the flight Freya turned to me and said *"Mummy, will you marry Daddy?"* I felt embarrassed that she had asked, as I was unaware that she knew her father and I weren't married, as it was never something we openly discussed. I had changed my surname by deed poll to ensure that Freya and I shared the same name, but somehow she understood that we weren't married. I replied, *"Maybe one day sweetheart."* Robert then pulled a ring box from his pocket and Freya said again, *"Mummy, will you marry Daddy?"*

Robert opened the ring box to reveal a solitaire engagement ring inside. *"Well, will you?"* he asked. I was stuck for words and found it difficult to believe what was happening, as marriage meant commitment and I never believed that Robert would make that vow. I said, *"Yes Freya, Mummy will marry Daddy"*. She smiled and helped her father to put the ring on my finger. The passengers on board the flight must have been in on their plan, as many let out a cheer when I accepted. Robert then opened his hand luggage and pulled out congratulations cards from our family and friends, which revealed that they too were in on his plan.

When we landed in France, our friends immediately noticed the ring on my finger, as Robert had also shared his plans with them. That evening we enjoyed a celebratory meal and a glass of champagne at a local restaurant. Freya's first family holiday was a huge success and one which we all enjoyed. The week passed quickly and before we knew it, it was time to fly home again.

Freya had lots of memories to return home with, so I was happy.

Once home Freya couldn't wait to tell everyone that her mummy and daddy were getting married, including her friends at playgroup. She was so happy at the prospect of being a bridesmaid and wearing a beautiful princess dress. Robert was in no rush to set a date, though, as I think for him, the commitment of being engaged was enough for him at that time. He always said that he wanted to get married, but that money was tight and we couldn't really afford a wedding. Poor Freya, I knew that she would have a long wait until she got to wear her bridesmaid dress.

So we continued with life, like every other couple, and I thankfully noticed a change in Robert following the engagement. Our relationship had at last turned a corner, and the following year, after many discussions, we decided to have a brother or sister for Freya. We felt another child would be good for Freya and help solidify and complete our family unit. I managed to conceive after just four months and when we both found out that I was expecting again, we were overjoyed. We shared our news with Freya, who was extremely happy at the prospect of having a baby brother or sister. Or should I say that Freya was over the moon to be getting a baby sister, as for her a brother was not an option.

It was a traumatic pregnancy because at twenty three weeks I fell down some wet steps at our friend's house. My fall wasn't elegant and I could tell by the immediate pain that something was wrong and I was petrified that something had happened to our child. I rested when I got home, in the hope that our baby would be alright. However I soon started to lose blood and our baby hadn't kicked for a while. Robert drove me to the hospital and after an examination and numerous tests, the Doctors informed me that there was a possibility that I may go into early labour. The placenta had been damaged in the fall, so they were concerned that our baby may not be receiving the correct levels of oxygen and nutrients. I was distraught as any mother would be, as I had already formed a strong bond with our unborn child.

I was signed off work for six weeks and instructed to have complete bed rest during that time. As part of our care plan, I had to visit the hospital twice a week for a Doppler ultrasound scan. Doctors used this to assess our baby's health and measure the blood flow in the umbilical cord and the baby's body. It was a scary time as we were warned that babies born before twenty-eight weeks gestation require a lot of medical intervention.

I did not want to lose our precious child, so I did all I could to nurture him/her. I attended regular Reiki treatments to de-stress myself and the baby and get my physical body back into a state of balance. I also made the most of my time at home to reassure our baby that everything was going to be alright. I told our child every day how much I loved him/her and made a promise that I would do all I could to ensure that he/she was safe. I played music to calm and soothe, sang songs and repeatedly stroked my baby bump, hoping that our baby would feel the vibrations of my loving touch and find them healing.

After six weeks, the Doppler scans illustrated positive results, so reluctantly I returned to work. I kept reminding myself that it wouldn't be for long, as I was scheduled to leave work on Christmas Eve. I had pre-booked annual leave between Christmas and New Year, so that I could start my maternity leave on 2nd January. I planned it that way, so that I could make the most of my last month with Freya before our baby was born and because she started primary school in the New Year, too. I had consciously spent lots of quality time with her whilst I was pregnant as it was important to me that she didn't feel pushed out or rejected in any way. We especially enjoyed our Sunday mornings at the local cinema, watching their Kid's Club movie specials.

It was Freya's last Christmas as an only child, so we made it extra special for her. We intended for Freya's room to be the nursery, as it was the smallest room in the house, so we decorated the spare room as Freya's new bedroom. This was a surprise for Freya in addition to her Christmas presents. Her room was decorated in the theme of a princess castle and we had considered every detail. The walls were stone effect, she had a bespoke bed canopy with drapes, a hand-carved wooden wardrobe, a magic mirror above the open fireplace and a large gold key to get into her princess room. I knew that the thought of Santa coming down the chimney into her bedroom every Christmas Eve would excite Freya and we weren't disappointed with her reaction on Christmas Day. Her new room was a huge success.

After Christmas, Freya started primary school and I felt truly blessed to be able to drive her to and from school each day. She was an intelligent and sociable child, who always had a smile on her face and a twinkle in her eyes. Freya was more than ready to start school, as she yearned for additional mental stimulation as well as a broader social spectrum. I was extremely proud of the way that she embraced school and settled in so well. I felt being on maternity leave allowed her the stability to start school in a settled and calm way, and provided an important routine, and consistency.

My due date soon arrived, along with my appointment to attend hospital and see my consultant. The staff at the hospital believed that my placenta was compromised and could be damaging to our child, so they were reluctant for me to go even a day over my due date. The doctors explained that their preference was to induce me that day, which in my heart, I was fully expecting.

I wanted to see Freya before the hospital staff induced me, so that she was aware of what was happening and felt involved in the experience. I left hospital and collected Freya from school and explained that it was finally the day that we would get to meet her baby brother or sister. She was incredibly excited and kindly helped me to put my bags in the car for hospital. We travelled to the hospital and Freya helped settle me into my bed. I wanted her to be familiar with the hospital, its wards and equipment, so that she'd feel relaxed when she visited the next day. After a while, Robert took Freya for an overnight stay at her grandparents' house, whilst my mother remained in hospital with me.

The midwife was aware that I didn't want to be artificially induced, so allowed me to take homoeopathic remedies to naturally induce my labour. She warned me, however, that if my contractions didn't start within two hours they would have to review the situation. I took the remedies and walked the corridors in order to bring on my labour and thankfully, within just a few hours, I experienced contractions. Robert soon returned, so was in time to move from the side ward into the delivery room with me. The labour was very different to Freya's and our beautiful baby boy was born within a few hours of my contractions starting.

Having spent fourteen weeks worrying about whether he was going to be okay or not, I was overcome with emotion as I held Drew in my arms. I stared at our little miracle, who had battled so triumphantly for his place in our world, and felt overwhelmed with love, respect and adoration. I was immensely relieved to be able to finally hold him and grateful that he was safe. I know some mothers worry that they may not love their second child as much as their first, but I believe that worry disappears as soon as you hold your newborn in your arms. I didn't think it was possible for the human heart to hold such love, but that day I experienced my heart expand further. I was truly blessed to have been gifted two innocent and beautiful souls who would change my life for the better.

Thankfully, Freya was pleased to meet her baby brother and didn't want to send him back. It was incredible to witness the instant love and connection between them. Drew gave Freya a 'thank you for being my big sister' present when she arrived at the hospital. Freya wished that Drew didn't have to stay in hospital and asked when he was allowed home. Luckily she didn't have long to wait for her wish to be granted, as we left hospital that day.

Robert seemed a little anxious when we arrived home and wanted little physical interaction with Drew. He had been so hands on with Freya, and I'd automatically expected him to be the same with Drew. He seemed disinterested, not even offering to change his nappy. I was worried that on some level Robert was rejecting Drew, so I expressed my concerns to my midwife. She reassured me that some men find it difficult when another male comes into their house and territory, so to be patient and give Robert time to adjust.

I gave Robert the time and space he needed, whilst I focused on being a good mother to my two children. I knew that my maternity leave would soon pass and I would be returning to my full-time job, so I made the most of my time with them. It was perfect being a stay at home mum, having the time to cook homemade meals, clean the house and take the children out. Freya thought it was brilliant that her baby brother accompanied me on the school run every day and insisted on repeatedly showing him to her school teachers, as well as her swimming instructors, dance teachers and rainbow leaders. It was evident how much Freya loved her brother, how proud she was of him, and how much she enjoyed being a big sister.

15

The Bells Are Gonna Chime

When Drew was just seven weeks old, Robert came home from work and broadcasted, without discussion, that we were getting married. He informed me that he had already booked the venue and I had just five weeks to plan the wedding. I was gobsmacked, as his announcement was completely out of the blue and out of character. We hadn't discussed getting married since the engagement.

My mother put me on an immediate diet, as I was still carrying a lot of baby weight and then she set to task on organising the wedding. With such limited time, the first thing we had to do was choose a dress. Sadly, dress choices were restricted, as only a few bridal designers could guarantee delivery within five weeks. However, I managed to find the perfect cream dress with a fitted lace-up bodice, so it wouldn't require any alterations when it arrived. Dress ordered, it was time to focus on other arrangements.

Along with little time to organise the wedding, we also had very little funds. Therefore, we purchased off the peg bridesmaids dresses for Freya and my maid of honour, who was my best friend from college. Freya was certainly pleased with hers, it made her feel like a princess. Next stop was the photographers, followed by the florist, the chef to discuss menu options and finally outfits for the rest of the wedding party. Every day there was another task to fulfil and I wondered if we were going to get everything done in time.

Whilst co-ordinating arrangements, I decided that it was necessary to create hand-made invitations and bake and decorate the wedding cake myself. This meant that we could use our limited resources on the essentials. Robert's best friend and best man kindly paid for a designer suit for Robert. My best friend arranged to be my chauffeur to the register office and the wife of the best man planned to chauffeur us in her convertible Mercedes from the ceremony to the venue. This removed the need and cost for wedding cars. I was extremely grateful to everyone for being so generous and helpful.

The day before the wedding, I went to collect my dress from the bridal boutique. Upon arrival they presented me with my dress, but I immediately noticed that it was the wrong colour. I'd ordered my dress in cream but it had been made in an ivory fabric. I was mortified, as my flowers, the cake and the men's shirts were all coordinated in cream. An ivory dress would spoil the overall look of the wedding. I was so upset and just wanted to get it sorted, so I phoned Robert who was at the wedding venue, preparing it for the wedding. I cried inconsolably to him down the phone, hardly making much sense to him at all. He left the venue and drove to the bridal boutique to speak to the owner, but with the wedding scheduled for the next day, she was unable to get another dress in time. The only solution she was able to offer was an off the peg dress in cream.

My option was a separate skirt and top, which was a size 14, and hence two sizes too big. The owner arranged for a seamstress to alter the dress at an additional cost. Time was against us as the lady only had an afternoon to complete all the alterations. I knew that I had to compromise, so I accepted the off the peg one and convinced myself that it didn't matter in the grand scheme of things. It was simply a dress after all, and what truly mattered was the fact that we were getting married. We were going to become lawfully wedded and vow to forsake all others, which was really important to me, as this was Robert's public declaration that he would be faithful.

I awoke on the day of the wedding really nervous, but with a twelve week old baby and five year old to look after whilst getting ready, I didn't have much time to reflect on my nerves. We arrived at the register office for our intimate wedding of just fifteen guests. Everyone was in the room waiting for me, but, at the moment when I had to walk into the marriage room I froze. I announced to my uncle who was giving me away, that I couldn't go through with it. The registrar's assistant heard and offered me a glass of water, whilst my uncle assertively reminded me that I had two children with Robert and so there was no turning back; I had to go through with it. So I took a deep breath, sucked in my doubts and walked into the room. It was interesting that during the vows, I shook my head as I said, *"I do"*. An unconscious action, but one which spoke a thousand words.

The remainder of the day went to plan; the photographer took some great shots, the wedding breakfast and evening buffet was delicious and the magician went down a treat with the children in the evening. Our friends enjoyed amusing Freya and caring for Drew whilst Robert and I socialised with the 160 guests who'd joined in the celebration. At the end of the evening, we were all exhausted and ready to go home to bed.

There's a saying that 'true love never runs smooth' and our journey together certainly had its ups and downs. However, we were now a legitimate family. I loved Robert dearly and saw our marriage as a fresh start for us all. After all, we were blessed with two adorable children, had a nice home and both had good careers. Many people dream of having children, but are sadly denied the opportunity, many want the security of their own home, but, for whatever reason can't, and some would like a secure career, but maybe circumstances don't permit. I was truly grateful for all that we had achieved and I prayed that we had put the worst behind us and could now concentrate on creating a happy, loving home for our children.

Following the wedding, we made the most of my maternity leave before I had to return to work. I struggled to cope with the stress of such a demanding full-time role, with two young children at home. Travelling up and down the country with overnight hotel stays each month was extremely arduous, as I just wanted to be at home with my children. When I was at work I felt guilty for leaving my children and believed that somehow I was failing them as a mother. Then when I was at home, I felt guilty for not putting in extra hours at work, and so felt inadequate at my job. In my heart, I wanted to be a full-time mother to my children, as it was the role which gave me the most satisfaction, as well as enormous pleasure, fulfilment and happiness.

Within just a few months of returning to work, the company that I worked for luckily announced that they were making redundancies, so I put myself forward as a potential candidate. With no other job lined up, this was a risky decision as I earned a substantial wage and we relied upon my income to run the family home. Emotionally it was also tough, as the company had been my only employer since leaving university, and had become my work family. I knew, however, that this was the right decision long-term and would benefit us all.

I was soon offered a part-time job as a personal assistant at a local mortgage brokers. The pay was good and the hours were perfect, enabling me to drop Freya at school each morning and collect her from school too. Drew was registered at the same private day nursery that Freya had once attended, for two days per week, and Robert's parents agreed to care for him on the other three days. My substantial redundancy package bridged the gap in my wages for a while, so I felt that everything had worked in our favour.

For the first time ever, I had a work life balance which enabled me to spend quality time with the children and create more happy memories. I felt at peace and content. Maybe being married was the turning point we needed. Life now offered me some stability and the cycle of abuse which had previously played out in our relationship seemed to have come to an end, or so I thought.

16
Living Hell

Just after Drew's first birthday, Robert gradually began to return to his old invalidating ways and controlling behaviours. He once again became absent from family life, often returning from work late or working on his days off. When he received his payslip each month, however, he would hide it away, which I never understood. His actions created uncertainty in me and I often wondered if he was working overtime when he claimed to be.

His nights out with friends became more frequent and he went on an increasing number of holidays abroad with them. After a night at the dogs, I found a slip of paper in his jeans pocket with a lady's name and phone number on it. I went upstairs to have a bath, so that the sound of the running water would disguise the sound of a telephone call from our hands free phone. When the lady answered, I introduced myself and asked if she knew my husband. She immediately hung up the phone. I called back but this time her husband answered. I introduced myself again and informed him that I had found a piece of paper in my husband's jeans with his wife's name and number on it, and was calling to find out why. He told me to leave it with him. I never heard from either of them again.

After that, our relationship continued to grow increasingly tense until one day my whole world came crashing down around me. Our DVD player had broken and a friend of ours had advised us that Sainsbury's currently had a great offer on DVD players, and that it might be worth us having a look. It was a Saturday and Robert's day off work, so he was reluctant to leave the house on his day of rest. He agreed to look after the children for half an hour whilst I went to the supermarket, as I would be far quicker on my own. He handed me his mobile phone, as I didn't own one, and told me to call him when I got there, so that he could check I purchased the right model.

I grabbed my bag, said goodbye to the children, got in the car and drove the short trip to Sainsbury's. Upon arrival, I made my way to the electrical aisle and found the DVD players that were currently on offer. I took the mobile phone from my handbag so that I could call Robert to ensure it was the correct make and model. I switched on the phone and the screen opened on a recent call list showing that Robert had made calls to someone called Lisa. The only Lisa that I could think of was a mum at school whose daughter I sometimes looked after. Why would Robert be calling her?

I felt sick in the pit of my stomach, my legs turned to jelly and the next thing I knew, I had collapsed like a rag doll in the supermarket aisle. As my body hit the floor, I hid my head in my hands and sobbed. It was like I was being swallowed by a black hole, as everything around me faded into the distance and I was only conscious of my own body. I heard a voice ask, *"Are you okay? Can I help you?"* It was the voice of the supermarket security guard who was standing next to me. I could see and hear him, but I was unable to answer him. My mind had the ability to think the words, *"I'm okay, thank you,"* but my lips were paralysed and unable to speak. He asked me again, *"Are you okay?"*

I don't fully understand what happened next, as I was still in a state of shock, but I heard another voice whisper, *"You and the children will be fine. You are all strong."* I snapped out of my trance-like state and once again became conscious of the reality of what was happening around me. I wiped my eyes, told the security guard that I was fine and thanked him for his concern. He kindly helped me to my feet and I made a rapid exit from the store, mostly through sheer embarrassment. As I walked back to the car, my breath became shallower and more rapid and I could feel my heart beating loudly in my chest. These symptoms were familiar and a regular occurrence, as I had suffered with panic attacks for a few years. My vision became blurred and my lips tingled; I was scared.

I needed help, so I immediately called my best friend Rachael, who I could always rely upon. We had been best friends since sixth-form College and were always there for each other in times of crisis. I did my best to explain to her what had happened, but she struggled to understand me through my wailing, so she told me to get in the car and drive to her house and we would sort it when I got there. I am unsure how I managed to drive to Rachael's house, but I did. I somehow buried my emotions and composed myself enough to be able to drive, although it felt as if the car was driving itself. As soon as I pulled the car into her drive, she opened the front door, and I could see the concern in her eyes, which instantaneously made me breakdown in tears, so she embraced me and gave the supportive hug I craved.

Rachael didn't seem surprised by my news, but then again why would she be? She had been a passenger on my roller coaster ride with Robert. I could see that she was disappointed though, as like me, she thought that Robert may calm down after we had Drew and got married. Rachael said that I had to be sure, as it could be innocent and she was right, of course, as maybe I was jumping to the wrong conclusions.

To me, though, Robert and innocent were two words which were never present in the same sentence when it came to women. Rachael reached over the table and held my hand in sympathy and support. I took a deep breath to give me courage and I texted

Lisa from Robert's phone pretending to be him. Lisa soon texted back, so I engaged in sending several more texts. I shocked myself at how devious I was being, but I was in self-preservation mode and doing what was necessary to survive.

It was evident that something was going on between them, it was just unclear what that was. So I decided it was probably best to telephone her, so that I could get clarity. Rachael helped me to compose myself, so that I could speak to Lisa calmly. Lisa was expecting to hear Robert's voice when she answered the phone, so was shocked when she heard my voice say hello and immediately hung up.

I realised from her voice that it wasn't Lisa, the mum from school but Lisa who had been my friend and work colleague for five years. I was utterly devastated to be betrayed not only by my husband, but also my friend. *"How could they do this to me,"* I screamed. I called Lisa back in the hope that she would answer the phone and talk to me, but I guess it was no surprise that she would not answer my call. I pressed redial and tried again, but Lisa allowed the phone to go to answer machine. It became obvious that she wasn't going to answer so I left her a really calm message stating that I wanted to talk and that I couldn't understand why, as my friend, she had hung up on me. I then received a text to say that she was in the cinema so couldn't speak. I thought this was an odd excuse as she had answered the phone to me a few minutes previously and there was no cinema noise in the background of the call. I texted back to say I had to talk to her urgently, but I didn't get a reply.

Lisa never did call back but then again, why would she? I wanted to speak to her before I spoke to Robert, so that I could see if their stories matched but that wasn't to be. I now had to make a plan and decide what I wanted to do. My maternal instinct kicked in and I wanted to get my children out of our family home and with me, so that I knew they were safe. I called Robert and with a very convincing Oscar winning performance, told him that the DVD players were sold out and that I was just going to pop to Tracey's house with the kids so that they could play with Poppy and James. He believed me but then again, why wouldn't he? He had no idea that he had been found out.

So I drove from Rachael's back home, put the children in the car and then drove back again. She was my rock that day, and I will always be grateful to her for her support and friendship. Rachael played with the children in the living room and watched television with them, whilst I went upstairs to call Robert.

When Robert answered the home phone, I told him that I knew about Lisa and that he had an hour to pack his things and leave the house, so that I could go back home and get the kids fed and ready for bed. Robert used his usual tactic of denial and said, *"Know what?"* *"I know about you and Lisa,"* I replied. The phone went very quiet. After a long silence, Robert said, *"I don't know what you're talking about."* I was unbelievably calm in my response and told him that he wasn't going to lie his way out of this one and repeated that he had an hour to pack his bags and leave the house before the kids and I came home. He asked, *"What are you on about?"* so I simply repeated myself again and asked him not to argue. I had no energy to argue with him, as the life had drained out of me. I then ended the call.

I had cried so much over the years that my eyes had no more tears to cry. I came off the phone feeling numb, but somehow found an inner strength for the sake of my children, whom I loved and adored so much. Their wellbeing was my priority. I put on my happy face, went downstairs and played with Rachael and the children. After 15 minutes, there was a knock at the door. It was Robert. He had guessed that I had gone to Rachael's house and had come to talk, but I didn't want to see him, let alone talk to him. My heart began to beat loudly in my chest and my breathing quickened. I could feel a panic attack coming on. I told Rachael that I didn't want to speak to him and asked her to send him away. She answered the door and advised Robert that it was probably best to leave us alone for a while, so that I could calm down, and that it wasn't a good idea to talk in front of the children. Robert said that he wasn't leaving until he had spoken to me.

Rachael came back inside and continued playing with the children so that I could speak to Robert alone outside, as we didn't want to cause a scene. I asked Robert to keep his voice down, as I didn't want the children or Rachael's neighbours to hear. Robert begged me to tell him what I was talking about, as he didn't know what was going on. I explained that I had seen his mobile call list and that I had been in contact with Lisa. The blood drained from his face and he turned as white as a sheet, telling me that it wasn't what I thought. I told him that my friend in the police was sending off the telephone SIM card on Monday so that I could get a copy of the text messages and shed light on what had been going on. Robert's eyes widened, his breath quickened and I could see sheer panic on his face. In that moment, his body's response to what I had said confirmed to me that they hadn't just been exchanging innocent text messages. What had happened though was still unclear.

Robert said that he would do as I had asked and would pack his things, but only after we had put the kids to bed and talked. I didn't want to create a scene or cause any hassle for Rachael so I agreed. I thanked Rachael for her help and put the children in the car to take them home whilst Robert got back into his car. When we arrived home, the happy family act continued for the sake of the children. I robotically fed and bathed them, read them a bedtime story and put them to bed.

As soon as I could drop the pretence, I felt physically and emotionally exhausted. I made a cup of tea and went into the living room to talk to Robert. He was slumped on the sofa looking genuinely upset with his head in his hands, crying. Upset because of what he had done or upset because he had been caught out? Who knows? I told him that we were over and that we had to talk about how we were going to arrange the separation and divorce. He kept repeating that he hadn't done anything wrong and that he loved me and the children. I explained to him that it didn't matter anymore what he said, as on Monday I would find out the truth. I was bluffing of course, as my police friend wouldn't be able to get a copy of the messages, but Robert didn't know that. It was my ploy to get him to be honest with me, as I knew I had to force the truth out of him, as he would never volunteer it. As a pathological liar, Robert was always able to talk his way out of any situation.

It was then that he confessed to taking the phone whilst I was sorting out the children at Rachael's, and that he had thrown it in the local brook. I was horrified, as he had purposely destroyed any evidence of his infidelity. I shouted at him, *"Well, that was a really stupid thing to do because if nothing happened then you have just destroyed any evidence of your innocence."* Robert knew he wasn't innocent though, and so did I, in my head. I just didn't want to believe it in my heart, as I loved him.

We spent hours talking and went around in circles. It was like the floodgates had been opened and I poured out all of the things he had done over the years that had hurt me. The excuses came thick and fast. *"I wasn't ready to settle down then, but I am now; I didn't know that I loved you then, but I do now."*

Our conversations led nowhere and I was getting more frustrated and exhausted by the minute. What had I done wrong? Why did I deserve this? Why weren't the children and I enough for him? These were all the questions I had, but never got an honest answer to.

Seeing my frustration, Robert then announced that the texts and calls to Lisa were about his friend, Stuart. I asked him to explain why he would be calling her about Stuart, as surely Stuart was old enough to call her himself. I then posed the question that if the calls were innocent and about Stuart, why would Lisa have hung up when I called her? Robert wriggled out of my question by saying that he couldn't explain someone else's actions, which of course was true, he couldn't, but it didn't make sense to me, as she was my friend.

I had got to the point where whatever Robert did or said, I didn't trust or believe him. My heart had been broken so many times over the years, that a little piece of my heart had been chipped away with every incident and lie. I had invested all of me into our relationship and marriage, but for what benefit? My husband didn't love or respect me enough to be honest and faithful. I went to bed that evening feeling an utter failure and worthless.

Over the next few days, I pretended in front of the children that all was well in our family home. They didn't deserve to be hurt or feel pain because of the actions of their selfish father. My mind wouldn't switch off and I kept spinning Robert's many lies around in my head. I felt like I was going crazy with his generalisations and the uncertainty and doubt he'd created. So I decided to call his mobile phone provider, so that I could get a copy of the itemised bill. I couldn't keep spinning things in my head and I needed to prove matters one way or another for my own sanity. My gut instinct was telling me to leave Robert and end my suffering but my heart was telling me to give him another chance and stay. Without proof, I couldn't be a 100% certain and I needed evidence so that I could trust my own thoughts and feelings.

I called the mobile phone provider. The operator informed me that the telephone was registered in Robert's name, so he was unable to provide me with a copy of the itemised bill. I explained to the gentleman that my husband had bought the phone for me as a gift, and so he had registered it in his name upon purchase.

I asked if he could kindly email the itemised bill to Robert's email address, so that he was sending it to the registered owner of the phone. He agreed and emailed the bill to Robert.

Robert was at work, so I knew he wouldn't be accessing his emails. I logged onto his account and ten minutes later, the itemised bill was delivered to his inbox. I printed out the bill and highlighted with a pen, all of the calls and texts to Lisa's phone. I felt sick again, as there was a distinct pattern in the calls when he was working a night shift or at night after I had gone to bed. If Robert was genuinely calling her about his friend, then why didn't he text or make calls in front of me? She was my friend after all, so if trying to matchmake, surely he would have involved me? Alarm bells rang!

I started to look at specific dates and noticed that Robert had made calls to Lisa during the Easter weekend when he'd said he had to stay back at work. How could he have done that knowing that the children and I were waiting for him to go on a picnic in a nearby market town? They didn't exchange just a few texts, but pages worth, which would explain why my friend of five years hung up on me and never returned my calls. I called her again and this time she answered. I asked her to be honest and tell me what was going on but she said, *"If you want to know, then I suggest you ask your husband. Anyway, you know what he's like, he flirts with everyone!"*

How could my friend betray me like that, knowing he was married with children? How could Robert do this to me and the children? Enough was enough! I could no longer live my life going around in circles, as Robert slowly destroyed me. By staying in my marriage, I was giving him permission to continue his abuse. I deadlocked the front door so that he couldn't get in the house when he came back from work. I focused on the children and put my efforts into fulfilling their needs. My acting skills were getting better, as I was now able to suppress my emotions at will.

The children did not suspect anything was wrong, so we continued with life as normal that day.

Robert returned home from work and rang the bell as soon as he realised that his front door key didn't work. I composed myself before going to answer the door, and reminded myself of the voice in the supermarket that had reminded me I was strong. I opened the door calmly and said that we needed to talk. Robert looked confused, as if he didn't realise what we needed to talk about, conveniently forgetting the incident of only a few days earlier. I asked him to look me in the eyes and tell me honestly what had happened between him and Lisa. He said nothing, insisting he was calling her on behalf of his friend Stuart. I asked him again. He repeated his answer but added, *"I swear on the life of our kids"*. How could he swear on their lives, knowing that he was lying? It was then that I realised that my husband had no morals or values and would do anything to save his own skin.

So I asked him to tell me how many times he had texted or spoken to her? *"Oh, only a few times,"* was his reply. Knowing that he was lying, I repeated the question, but added that he needed to be honest. He repeated his answer with such conviction, that I would have believed him, had I not got a print out of the itemised bill. I asked him when he'd started texting her. *"Only a week or so before you found the messages."* I repeated the question again and asked him to be honest. He repeated his answer and said, *"I swear on the lives of our children."*

"You know everything Helen. I told you everything. Why are you doing this to me?" I couldn't believe that he had turned this around on me. He'd put himself in the position of victim and made me out to be the persecutor. How dare he swear on the lives of our beautiful and innocent children for his own gains? How low would this man sink to ensure he got his own way? I pulled out the itemised bill and screamed at him that he was lying. At that, Freya came into the room and asked what was wrong. I told

her, *"Mummy and daddy are just sorting something out, sweetie, and you should go to your room and play for a while."* Freya went up to her bedroom to play as instructed.

Robert looked horrified when he saw the itemised bill. His face went as white as a ghost's just like that day at Rachael's house. He also expressed the same look that he had that day when the police came to arrest him, as he knew everything was falling away from him and was out of his control. In his panic, Robert telephoned my mother and his mother and father to come to the house. How was he going to lie his way out of this one? Robert was metaphorically cornered, with nowhere to run and nowhere to hide.

I surprised myself at how composed I was when I told him that our marriage was over and that I wanted him to pack his things and leave. I believe my strength that day came from the previous six months of counselling which I had been regularly attending. My counselling sessions had helped me to release my belief that I wasn't good enough for Robert, that his actions were in some way my fault and that maybe he did those things because I was a bad person. With the help of my counsellor, I realised that Robert would never be satisfied with one woman, that his sick mind games were part of his personality and that he had a strong desire to hold the power in the relationship at any cost. I had also discovered that I was a good person. I was a loving mother to my children, I deserved happiness and I was strong enough to cope on my own.

When my mother arrived, she looked at Robert and asked, *"What have you done?"* She then proceeded to go upstairs to play with the children so that we could continue to talk. Within minutes, his mother and father arrived and sat with us in the front living room. Robert's mother asked, *"What on earth is going on?"* *"Go on, Robert, you can tell them what you've done."* I said. Robert couldn't catch his breath and struggled to speak. He insisted that all he had done was text another woman and promised that there was nothing in it. Robert's father looked exceedingly disappointed, as he was a kind man who was honest and true to his family.

I handed them the itemised telephone bill and explained that the lady he had been texting was Lisa, my friend. I then looked at Robert and asked him to explain to his parents why he had gone to so much trouble to hide the calls and texts from me, if he was genuinely trying to matchmake Lisa and Stuart. *"I was just stupid,"* was his lame and feeble excuse. I explained that our marriage was over and that Robert had to move out. His mother began to cry, held her chest and struggled to catch her breath. She sobbed, *"You don't mean that, Helen"*. I replied, *"Oh yes I do. This isn't the first time but it will certainly be the last."* *"Think of the children,"* she begged. *"Was Robert thinking of the children when he was with Lisa?"* I asked. She became more upset, so upset in fact that I was worried that she was going to have a heart attack. She continuously begged me to allow Robert to stay.

Concerned for his mother's wellbeing, I let Robert stay that evening, not because I wanted him to, but because it broke my heart to see his mother in so much pain. After all, she had done nothing wrong and was another casualty of Robert and his selfish actions. When everyone had gone home, he continued to insist that nothing had happened. *"I know what it must look like, but I promise nothing happened,"* he repeatedly told me. After an incident, Robert's routine was always to make a promise: *"I will do anything to make it up to you, I promise! I won't go out so much with the lads or go on holiday with them. I just want you and the children. You are my world."* However, a promise is just empty words if the person who makes it does not follow through with appropriate actions.

17

Last Chance Saloon

The following day, Robert was extremely remorseful and adopted a wounded posture, with his shoulders slumped and his head down. His voice became quiet and meek in order to further enhance his saddened façade. He grew increasingly submissive in his behaviour, as if he was the injured victim in this latest incident. This was Robert's pattern of behaviour when he had been caught out - invoking sympathy in the hope that all would be forgiven.

The reality was that Robert was an abuser and I was the innocent victim, but I loved him. I knew I was strong enough to cope on my own, but I didn't want to. I wanted to raise our two children together as a family and that was an ideal which I clung to. After further discussions, I agreed to give Robert a final chance but this time I made it quite clear to him that it was just that; his final chance. I emphasised to Robert that he had to adhere and follow through on his promises and warned him not to make any promises that he wasn't willing to keep.

I trusted that this latest incident gave Robert a genuine scare, as he had come so close to losing his family. It was now clear to Robert that I was willing to leave him and I believed that this was enough for him to change his ways and become a faithful husband. Although I wished more than anything for Robert to be honest and true, I still found it extremely difficult to trust him, as my heart had been shattered into a million pieces.

During the weeks that followed, I lived my life on tenter hooks every time his mobile phone beeped or rang. When he went out with his friends, I would worry about where he was and what he was doing. I wanted so desperately to put the past behind us and move on, so that we could enjoy being a family. I wanted the dramas to stop and the cycle of psychological abuse to cease, so that we could be a proper married couple. I wanted him to love me the way that I loved him.

Our crystal/glass wedding anniversary was approaching and yet I didn't feel like celebrating. The vows we took no longer meant anything to me and they felt like a bitter sweet pill to swallow. Robert, however, saw our anniversary as an opportunity for him to make amends and planned a surprise for me. He booked the restaurant where we held our wedding reception and arranged for the chef to recreate our wedding meal. My best friend decorated the table with the same flowers that I had in my wedding bouquet and arranged for us to drink the same wine that we had enjoyed on our wedding day. It was a romantic gesture and under different circumstances I would have been overjoyed at how thoughtful and romantic he was being. After recent events, though, I found it a challenge to see any kind sentiment in his actions and felt that it did not make up for his lies. It was wonderful that after all these years, Robert was at last making an effort, but my heart was closed to him, as I had promised myself that I would never allow him to hurt me again.

That evening was Robert's sticking plaster attempt at brushing his recent actions under the carpet, as he had refused point blank to properly talk about what had happened. However, without an open and honest discussion I couldn't fully comprehend why he had chosen to lie to me, nor could I understand why he had chosen to do what he did. Without a reason how would I know that he wouldn't feel compelled to do the same again? How could I fully trust him?

I had so many unanswered questions, which frequented my mind on a daily basis, and without proper answers I was struggling to move on. I asked Robert to attend couples counselling with me, so that we could put the past behind us and move forward. He surprisingly agreed, so we set up an appointment at the local counselling centre. Counselling had helped me so much in the past and I believed it was the solution to fix our relationship. It turned out to be a waste of time, as Robert did not take any responsibility for his actions and I didn't get any answers. Subsequently, we decided to stop going, which seemed to please Robert.

I did my best to preserve normal life for the sake of the children, but the mental and emotional strain became wearing for my physical body. I sought help from my doctor who prescribed antidepressants to help my ongoing panic attacks. I hated taking conventional medicine but couldn't see what else I could do, so I collected the medication from the chemist and went home. I looked at the packet of pills and wondered how my life had come to the point where I needed pills to cope. I felt mentally weak and pathetic again, but what choice did I have? None.

When I awoke the next day, I reluctantly took my first tablet, well actually it was my first and last. I was so used to taking alternative medicine that the chemicals made me feel light headed, nauseous and out of control. Antidepressants may work for some people, but they weren't the right solution for me, as they put me in a zombie-like trance. I threw the tablets away and instead sought a solution in a book loaned to me by my best friend.

Although I felt weak and pathetic, I knew that deep down I was capable of getting myself through my anxiety and panic attacks. I made a commitment to myself that I would put 100% effort into helping myself and that I would have a positive mindset about what I read and not allow my ego to be sceptical. I wholeheartedly applied the techniques as instructed in the book, and was consistent in my approach. I soon realised that the small persistent changes I made to the way I thought and behaved actually made me feel much better about myself and aided me in overcoming my panic attacks.

I also attended regular Reiki treatments with a Reiki Master Practitioner and teacher, who had been recommended to me by a friend. The Reiki sessions provided me with the opportunity to verbally offload my worries and concerns and let go of stress. With each treatment, I noticed significant improvements in my mental and emotional state, and for the first time in a long time, I felt in control of my own thoughts and feelings, as well as feeling balanced and content within myself.

18

A Wolf in Sheep's Clothing

Two years after my initial treatment, the Reiki Master asked if I wanted to learn Reiki, so that I could carry out self-healing treatments. I had already completed Reiki Level One and Two training before I gave birth to Drew, but sadly I hadn't used it much, so I saw his offer as an opportunity to reconnect with the knowledge and skills that I had previously learnt. Finances were still tight, so my mother kindly paid for the course for me as a birthday present.

Over the next twelve months, I went on to complete Level Two and Masters Certificates in *Usui Reiki,* as I found immense benefit in my self-healing treatments and from regularly working with energy healing. As part of my Reiki journey, I joined a Self-Development Program that my Reiki Master ran and also enjoyed his monthly group, which allowed me to connect with like-minded people. I began to make new friends, expand my spiritual interests and explore my own spiritual beliefs.

I continued to have one-to-one treatments with my Reiki Master, to address my past demons in private and banish them once and for all. Through my openness and honesty, he discovered my greatest weaknesses, vulnerabilities and Achilles' heel. He knew that I felt rejected and abandoned by my father, unworthy of my husband and that at work I had to fight to be seen as an equal in a male dominated industry. By selecting a male therapist, it was my intention that he would help me regain my faith and trust in men.

During a treatment one day, we worked on my ability to let go of past hurts in my relationships, something which most of us carry around subconsciously. The treatment was highly emotional and I sobbed for most of it, but by the end of the session I felt much lighter, as if burdens had been lifted. At the end of the session, I paid for the treatment, booked my next one and then went to leave, but as I did so my Reiki Master reached out and hugged me. He said, *"You do know I love you, don't you? You know that we would be together if I wasn't with my partner."* In that moment, my faith and trust in men completely disappeared; he had sexualised a platonic relationship and breached the boundary between a therapist and client. He had projected his own feelings about me onto me, assuming that I felt the same way about him. He had mistaken my trust in him for love and had completely misread the situation, which was that I was simply a person seeking help from a professional.

I felt completely betrayed again. I had been betrayed by my husband, my friend and now a supposed professional in his field. I am sure that it will be no surprise to learn that I did not return for further treatments, and I even contemplated reporting him, as he was using his position of trust inappropriately. I never did report him, but a few years later I regretted not taking action against him, as I learnt that I wasn't his only victim. Allegedly he had acted unprofessionally with other women too, on at least two occasions. He was a wolf in sheep's clothing, pretending to be a kind, thoughtful and helpful person when in fact he had his own seedy agenda. He used his profession as a secret mask to lure vulnerable women into his predatory trap and feed his own ego. I was astounded at how well he had conned so many people into believing that he was a genuine lightworker and how magnificently he had hidden his dark and sinister side.

The incident with my Reiki Master shattered my faith in spirituality for a while, as I didn't feel I could trust anyone. Every cloud has a silver lining however, and as a result of meeting him, I made friends with a lady who later became - and who continues to be - a very dear friend. If I hadn't trained with him, our paths may never have crossed.

Whilst the trauma was happening with my Reiki Master, I was also experiencing issues at work. As you know, it wasn't the first time I had experienced being bullied, and now, years later, it was happening again. The current managing director had started there as an employee before buying the company. Initially he was very welcoming and charming, but he soon revealed his true nature and characteristics. I don't believe that he would see his actions or words as abusive, as it was just the way he was, very old school. However, many of us were uncomfortable with his behaviour but hid our true opinions from him as we needed a job. At some time or another he was abusive to everyone by using the following methods:

- Humiliation to reprimand staff in front of others rather than in private.

- Emotional abuse to make an individual feel unworthy of the job, and therefore feel guilty. In reality, nothing was ever good enough unless he had done it himself, of course.

- Intimidating looks and gestures to criticise an individual's work.

- Blaming behaviour, as it was always someone else's fault when anything went wrong. He was incapable of taking personal responsibility.

- Economic abuse to make you feel grateful to him. For example, he would regularly remind staff that he paid their wages and that they were lucky to be on such a high rate of pay. This caused an individual to feel subservient and indebted to him.

- Use of other people's ideas as his own.
- Inappropriate physical gestures towards the women at work. For example, he slapped my posterior as I walked up the stairs one day.

I tolerated his behaviour as I needed the money. Robert's income alone was not enough to cover our bills or pay off the debts that he quickly accumulated on credit cards. Anyway, as an independent business, who was I going to complain to, as he was the owner? My tipping point at work came one day when Freya was ill and I called work to book a day's annual leave, so that I could stay at home and nurse her. I explained that although I was taking a day's annual leave, I would dial into the company computer network from home whilst Freya was sleeping and complete any urgent work remotely.

The following day Freya had returned to good health and went to school so I went to work as usual. Upon arrival, the managing director said that he needed to speak to me urgently. *"Don't you ever fucking do that again,"* he shouted.

"Do what?" I enquired.

"Take a day off work when your children are ill. Next time, you drop them at the childminders on your way to work.," he demanded.

"Childminders won't take children when they are ill. Surely your wife had to have the occasional day off when one of your four children were ill?" I enquired.

"No, as she was a proper mother. She didn't work." he smugly replied.

My heart sank, as he was implying that I was a substandard mother to my children. I was simply working to pay the bills and ensure that my children's needs were provided for. Unlike him, I didn't have the luxury of owning a business which had an annual turnover of more than £1,000,000. I struggled to make ends meet every month, as Robert was reckless with money.

I managed his company as if it were my own, making an annual saving in the first year alone in excess of my annual salary. I secured NVQ training courses for the staff at no cost to the business. In fact, he earned money from it as the training provider paid the company for the hours that the staff worked on their qualification. Of course, he pocketed the money for himself, instead of allocating some of it to the staff. That day I decided that I would no longer go above and beyond. No more arriving at work half an hour early or staying late, no more missed lunch breaks. I would only do what was legally required from me at work. Not long after, I then left the company, so that I could support Robert through his promotion.

I wondered why I seemed to attract abusive relationships. Upon reflection, I concluded that the only common connection was me, so in some way I must be to blame. My Reiki treatments had helped me, but as you know, they came to an end following the Reiki Masters' behaviour. I was now lost on where to go for help, so I confided in a close friend who was also an experienced therapist. She shared with me her experiences and wisdom and felt that in order for me to fully resolve and heal my issues, I needed to therapeutically address them physically, emotionally and mentally. She believed that I had only been addressing my challenges from one angle, which is why my health was so fragile. I realised that I had addressed the majority of my issues mentally, sometimes emotionally, but never physically. I had neglected the opportunity to heal my 'whole' self. How did I miss something which seemed so obvious?

So I assessed my approach to self-healing and made it my quest to find new methods and techniques that would enable me to heal my whole self. During this quest, I attended more courses, read more self-help books, went to seminars, tried new therapies and connected on a regular basis with others who believed in, and had a passion for, alternative medicine and healing.

This different approach resulted in great personal transformation. I felt stronger in myself, more self-assured and confident. My panic attacks ceased and my health improved, as I noticeably suffered from less headaches. I felt more in control of my life and was able to detach more readily from day-to-day dramas. I felt more grounded and able to make balanced decisions.

19

When Enough is Really Enough

M y story comes full circle and after much reflection following Drew's tipping point which, I outlined in Chapter One, I made my decision. Ironically, after years of psychological abuse and suspected adultery, it was not Robert's behaviour that prompted me to leave, but my two beautiful children; they were and are my saviours. I realised that by allowing myself to be a victim, I was condoning Robert's behaviour and by proxy teaching my children that abusive behaviour is acceptable and that being a victim is tolerable. By endorsing the cycle of abuse within my children's lives, I knew there was a possibility that they could go on to either be an abuser, or become a victim of one. That knowledge alone was the proverbial slap in the face I needed to wake-up and bring the abuse to an end.

This time, I would not allow Robert's parents or anyone else for that matter, talk me around or convince me to change my mind. I decided that enough really was enough and that I would no longer allow myself to be emotionally manipulated or psychologically abused. Robert could no longer use the children to make me feel guilty for splitting up our family, as it was his own actions that had done that. Whether he chose to take responsibility for that was his choice.

So, the week before Valentine's Day 2010, I told Robert that I wanted a divorce. He laughed and said, *"Of course you do."* I explained to Robert that I was serious this time and that I couldn't take it anymore. I was deeply unhappy and couldn't cope. He simply replied, *"Well fuck off then, but don't think you're taking the kids."* I told him that they certainly weren't staying with him but he angrily replied, *"If you think you're staying in this house, you can think again, as I'm not fucking supporting you, so what are you going to do?"*

Even at the point of separation, Robert's psychological abuse continued. He used the children as a means of power, and money as a means of control. Robert knew I had no income, as the previous year I had sacrificed my own career to support him in advancing his. I was a stay-at-home mum with no means of financially supporting myself or the children. However, his threats would not stop me from leaving, as money had lost its value to me. My sanity, wellbeing and children, however, were priceless.

Over the next seven months, I worked out how and when I could leave. I think Robert hoped that I would change my mind as I had done before, as he begged me not to tell the children that we were separating. He even asked two of his friends to tell me how devastated he was and how much he loved me. They tried to convince me to stay. What short memories Robert's friends had; had they forgotten how he had treated me over the years? I wondered if they would stay under the same circumstances.

He ill chose his messengers, as the first was on his second marriage, so I promptly reminded him of that and asked if he regretted leaving his first wife. Of course, he couldn't answer so his argument was blown out of the water. Robert's second messenger was his superior at work, who frequented prostitutes in favour of intimacy with his own wife. Neither of his friends could convince me that I was making a mistake by leaving Robert, and I found their reasons for staying laughable.

I knew Robert loved me in his own way, but it was not a way in which I wanted or needed to be loved. I wanted someone who could love me unconditionally, who adored me, found me attractive, enjoyed my company, could hold stimulating conversations with and could laugh *with me* not at me. I knew Robert's pride was hurting more than his heart, as he felt humiliated that I was ending the relationship, not him. His biggest fear had also become a reality; he could no longer control me.

During those months, I continued to live a lie, as only my close family and friends knew that I was planning to leave Robert. I would spend nights in the spare room when I could, and then move into our marital bed first thing in the morning before the children awoke. To make life bearable, I visited friends most weekends, so that Robert and I didn't have to be in the same house together. During the week, Robert didn't return home until at least 8pm most evenings, so we managed to be civil to each other until 9pm when the children went to bed.

At Robert's request, we even went on our August family holiday as planned, which I agreed to for the sake of the children who were still unaware that their mother and father were separating. September came and I was ready to tell the children, but Robert still didn't believe I would go through with it. Maybe he believed it was an idle threat or that I would change my mind as I had done before. Who knows?

I knew that staying was no longer an option, as if I did I would either go insane or commit suicide. I had contemplated suicide on so many occasions before, but never with the intention of going through with it, as I would never leave my children. I stuck to my plan and found a rented house in the same village, so that the children could continue at their existing schools, which would give them some level of consistency. I planned to either get a suitable part-time job or become a self-employed therapist.

Whatever happened, I knew in my heart that the children and I would be looked after and our needs would be met. We didn't need much money as we had each other. So long as I could provide a warm, safe house and feed them, I was happy.

When it came to telling the children, I felt sick to my core. Robert insisted that I told them, as it was my decision to split up the family, not his. He turned on the tears for the benefit of the children, in the hope that they would take his side, and told them that he didn't want me to leave and that it was my decision. He cleverly absolved himself of all blame. That day is not a day I ever want to repeat again, as it broke my heart seeing the devastation on the children's faces, but I kept reminding myself of why I was leaving and that one day they would understand.

"I learned that courage was not the absence of fear, but the triumph over it. The brave man is not he who does not feel afraid, but he who conquers that fear." ~ Nelson Mandela

---

On 10th October 2010, I conquered my fears and moved out of the family home and into my new one with the children. It was the day that I obtained my freedom! Robert remained in the family home with all our furniture and possessions, so he was happy. The children and I moved into our new home with just our clothes, their toys and little more. Kind friends donated bed linen, towels, cutlery, dinner service, and a television. Luckily, my landlord gave me a sofa, a dining room table and chairs, a washing machine and a fridge freezer, so my immediate priority was just beds. We may not have had much, but it was ours. Possessions meant very little to me, as they were just items which could be replaced, having no real emotional significance or value. I had exercised true detachment. I am not a religious person, but for the first time ever I could relate to a passage in the bible which states:

"For we brought nothing into the world, and we can take nothing out of it." ~ 1 Timothy 6:7

At the time, I believed that leaving was the hard part and was ill prepared for what was to follow. I could somehow cope with the legal battle and Robert's refusal to financially support his children, as his behaviour was exactly how I expected it to be. However, not being able to see my children every day tore me apart and still does today. I was ill prepared for the treatment I would receive from parents at the school. When collecting Drew from the school gates, parents would avoid eye contact with me or ignore me point blank.

No one knew why I left Robert as I chose not to tell anyone in the village about the psychological abuse I had endured, in case this information got back to my children. Yet, it seemed that people had come to their own conclusions, seeing Robert as the victim and me as the persecutor. One lady even cooked meals for him and introduced him to her friend as a possible suitor. At that time I realised just how judgemental human beings can be. Other than immediate family and close friends, I felt extremely isolated and alone.

20

Time For Change

I decided it was time to reconnect with like-minded individuals. A close friend recommended a spiritual group run by a lady called Sarah who was well known locally and who had been working with Reiki for many years. From our brief discussion, I thought Sarah sounded an ideal teacher, so I attended her monthly Reiki Share group to see if I connected well with her. The room was filled with approximately twenty people, which was a good level of attendance for such an event.

Throughout the evening there was something about her that I didn't feel comfortable with, but I couldn't put my finger on what that was. I decided to repress and dismiss my feelings, as with so many followers, I felt my doubts were unfounded. Over our next few meetings, I repeatedly had an uneasy feeling about her, a feeling I recognised and yet couldn't clearly identify. I assumed my instincts were misguided, due to my emotional state.

I commenced with the healing sessions with Sarah and decided to retrain in Usui Reiki Level One and Two, as well as completing my Masters. I felt that my previous Reiki Master had contaminated the energy with his inappropriate conduct. I later learnt, however, that my first Reiki Master was a student of Sarah, which explained the familiar uncomfortable feeling I experienced when we first met. They both had very similar energy.

Our relationship grew and as well as being my Reiki Master and teacher, Sarah became my friend. I invested a lot of time and love into our friendship, gave her support and a home retreat when her relationship ended. I took her to a weekend spa and gifted money to her animal charity. I trusted, respected and loved her dearly. Then one day, her attitude towards me promptly changed when I expressed an interest in becoming a Master Teacher myself.

Her change in behaviour confused me until someone highlighted to me that whilst she may have trained many people in Reiki over the course of her career, only a handful had gone on to establish successful businesses. This knowledge gave me a different perspective and allowed me to reconnect with my initial feelings. She was another wolf in sheep's clothing, using the mask of spirituality and charity to gain followers and exploit their generosity.

I remembered a conversation she'd had with me one day when we were close. She confessed to me that she felt like a fraud, as she took money from people to teach them about Reiki, the Law of Attraction and Money Mastery and yet she lived in a mobile home in constant struggle. She hid this fact from clients and students, as she knew it was hypocritical to portray herself as a master when in reality she hadn't truly learnt the art of self-mastery. At the time, I reassured her that we all experience difficulties at some time or another and not to be so hard on herself.

However, when I found myself to be the target of her ego, I realised that her words that day were truthful. She only allowed people to see the aspects of her that she wanted them to see, so that they would put her on a pedestal. She wasn't living authentically. I am sharing this with you simply to highlight the following:

- The need to trust your own inner guidance, irrespective of what others perceive.

- If something doesn't feel right, walk away without justification.

- There is good and bad in every profession and healers are no different. Work out for yourself who is right for you.

- Never judge a book by its cover, as everything is not always as it seems. Look beyond a person's mask.

- Be a shepherd, not a sheep. There is never a need to tread in some else's crap.

During a time of feeling isolated and alone, I had allowed myself to be a sheep and follow the crowd, instead of allowing myself to be my own shepherd. My experience with Sarah was heart breaking at the time, but I have no regrets, as throughout our relationship I always acted from my heart, showed kindness and was genuine. My Reiki Master decided to evict me from her community for completing my Master Teacher training with another teacher. Her actions during the months that followed, and which continue today, demonstrate her true personality. She has far to go in order to become a true Master, as her behaviour was cruel, her tongue was vicious and her public comments were slanderous. However, I forgive her as none of us are perfect and we can all make mistakes.

"When the student is ready, the teacher will appear."
~ *Buddhist proverb.*

Having been through so many abusive relationships, I couldn't believe that I had attracted yet another one when I felt that I was

139

making such progress in my personal development. I soon realised, however, that I had changed my mindset when it came to personal relationships, but I had not changed it when it came to my own abilities. There was still an aspect of me which was running the old program that 'I wasn't good enough' and so I looked up to others in their career, as I believed that I was incapable of such success. In putting another human being on a proverbial pedestal, I had briefly returned to 'victim mode' by classing myself as less capable. I quickly recognised how I was feeling and the way I was being treated, so chose to remove myself from the situation for my own wellbeing. Upon reflection, I realised that I had learnt a valuable lesson; instead of allowing myself to be psychologically abused for 15 years like I had done with Robert, I now valued myself enough to bring an end to the abuse within a matter of months. My relationship with Sarah enabled me to truly value myself, my skills and the service I gave to others through my business.

When I removed myself from that particular spiritual community, I made space for new people to enter my life, and they did. I connected with various spiritual people all over the world who truly acted from the heart. They lived their life in the universal flow of abundance and unity consciousness, as well as genuinely walking their talk. They have all rebuilt my faith in spirituality and I thank them from the bottom of my heart for that. They have shown me that those who are truly spiritual are humble and demonstrate humility, which allows the beauty of their heart to radiate from them like a sunbeam. Those with pure hearts and intent truly empower others to reconnect with their own personal power, encouraging them to be their true selves and to experience prosperous lives. I feel truly blessed to be part of a genuine community of people who empower others to succeed, so that we can evolve and make positive changes in the world.

21

Lessons Learnt

I had been stripped of my identity as Robert's wife, and so it was time to discover who I was and re-build myself. The real 'Helen' was buried so deep that it took me a while to reconnect with her, believe and ultimately trust her. I was gentle, kind and patient with myself during this journey to self-realisation. Some days were easier than others, but every day I reminded myself that I was worth the struggle, and 'doing my best' was good enough.

When I look at myself in the mirror I see a very different person from the one I used to be, as I have changed beyond recognition. My inner journey has helped me grow and evolve in ways I never dreamed of, and I have been blessed with miracles along the way. I am truly awake and enjoy an increased level of awareness which enables me to live life in an enlightened way.

Whilst visiting my friend in London recently, her mother commented on a conversation we were having: "*When therapists get together, I suppose it's natural for them to analyse everything,*" she said. I found her statement interesting as I don't see discussions as analytical but as opportunities for learning on both sides. I went on to explain the following analogy.

When I look at a painting, I instantly know if I like it or not, but if asked to comment I have very little to say other than to describe what I see and perhaps talk about the use of colour. If an artist views the same painting, he/she would be able to comment on the mood of the painting, the composition, use of materials, etc. That is because an artist views a painting from a different level of awareness. This can be said for other areas of life, too.

Therefore, I asked my friend's mother to think about whether we were analysing during our conversation or simply coming from a different level of awareness. When a person's level of self-awareness changes, one naturally has an increased awareness of others and their behaviours. I feel this is the key to choosing balanced friendships and the secret to benefitting from fulfilling relationships.

Relationships are integral to all areas of our lives: school, college, work, family, friends, our partners, and then one day maybe our own children. An increased level of awareness in relationships therefore helps one to:

- Come from a place of understanding.
- Have empathy with others.
- Understand your own needs.
- Understand the needs of others.
- Be able to compromise.
- Be balanced in giving and receiving.
- Discern when old emotional patterns are being triggered.
- Encourage each other to be individuals.
- Value codependency.
- Connect through a scared heart.

When I had a low level of self-awareness, I faced many subconscious challenges which I struggled to move beyond because I didn't have the tools to do this.

These included:

PHYSICALLY

- Suffering from regular headaches, adrenal fatigue, panic attacks, depression.

MENTALLY

- Being stuck in old negative programming and thought patterns.
- Repeated unhealthy patterns of behaviour.
- Fear of rejection.
- Codependency.

EMOTIONALLY

- Being connected to my wounded child.
- Trust issues.

SPIRITUALLY

- Being trapped in victim consciousness.
- Carrying negative etheric cords.
- Unresolved karmic bonds.
- Feeling disconnected from others.

My inner journey and increased awareness has helped me learn:

PHYSICALLY

That I am responsible for my own health. The same mind/body which creates disease, is also capable of healing it.

MENTALLY

That I am responsible for my own mental health. The mind is an extremely powerful tool and one that we should learn to use as our ally. 90% of our thinking is subconscious and often controls our thoughts and automatic behaviours. Our mind can be re-programmed and updated at any time we choose.

EMOTIONALLY

That I am responsible for my emotional health. My emotions are an inner satnav to how I feel about someone or something. How I choose to act upon my emotions is my responsibility and choice. There are no negative emotions as we are here to experience the whole spectrum. For example, if I feel angry about something, I listen to what the anger is telling me. For instance, it may be that something has happened which is outside of my core values. Therefore, anger is a healthy response. However, if I choose to outwardly express that anger by shouting at or hitting another, then my expression of anger would be inappropriate. If I choose to outwardly express that anger by channelling it into something good, then this would be a healthy expression of the emotion.

SPIRITUALLY

That I am responsible for my spiritual health. I chose to refer to this aspect of myself as my spirit, but it is also known by other names such as soul, universe, or spark.

By expanding my level of awareness, I have realised the importance of unity consciousness, respect for nature and all living things, and I believe I am the co-creator of my own reality. I work with the Universal Laws in order to live consciously.

All that I share with you would be meaningless unless I illustrated to you how much my life has changed as a result of changing myself. I guess the proof is always in the pudding, so you may be curious to know what I'm doing now. I am pleased to announce that I enjoy a wonderful relationship with my two beautiful children, whom I love and respect so much. My relationship with my mother is stronger than ever and she continues to be my best friend and rock. I am blessed to have my oldest and dearest friend nearby and we continue to be there for each unconditionally. I have also formed new friendships, which I cherish, as they are real and authentic friends; one is my best friend and walking companion in the village and the other is the mother of my godson. I have realised that distance doesn't matter when it comes to friendships and thanks to modern technology I am able to connect regularly via social media and video calls with friends who are further afield.

On a personal level, I connected with my soulmate. It was refreshing to meet someone who instantly liked me for simply being me. Our relationship initially started as a friendship, as we had much in common and felt at ease with each other from the onset. I later learnt, during a past life regression session, that we had shared past lives together, which explained why we felt so comfortable in each other's company.

Scott is like no other man I have ever met. He is exceptionally kind, thoughtful, considerate and romantic. He is genuine, sincere and honest and with him, what you see is what you get. He was exceptionally patient with me in the beginning of our relationship and helped me to overcome my trust issues.

He accepts my quirky ways, demonstrates unconditional love for my children and me and encourages me to be the best I can be. Today, I am proud to call him my husband.

Part Two

How to Achieve Self-Realisation

22
Knowledge is Power

I feel it necessary to start this part of the book by firstly defining what is considered as abuse or abusive behaviour. This is in order to avoid any misunderstanding or misrepresentation. Abuse is a harsh word and I feel it's one, which over the years, has mainly been identified with acts of physical or sexual violence. I would like to suggest, however, that you remove all preconceived ideas about what you consider as abuse, and I invite you to redefine its meaning for yourself. How you define abuse and abusive behaviour will go hand in hand with your own beliefs, core values and personal boundaries, as only you can decide what is acceptable or not for you personally. Once you have clearly defined this for yourself, you will be able to easily recognise abusive behaviour in everyday life.

According to the Collins dictionary terms, abuse means:

1. Prolonged ill-treatment of, or violence towards someone.

2. Insulting comments.

3. Improper use: an abuse of power.

So what is classified as 'ill-treatment'? According to the Collins dictionary it means:

To treat cruelly or harshly.

Cruel is another unforgiving word and one that we classify as being a physical act. However, if we widen our perspective, we can appreciate that people also inflict mental and emotional cruelty on others, which can also be referred to as psychological abuse. We must take into account, however, that what one person may perceive as cruelty or cruel behaviour, another may consider acceptable. This may be due to our upbringing, personal core values and varying levels of emotional intelligence.

Cruel as an adjective which, according to the Collins dictionary, means:

> *Wilfully causing pain or suffering to others, or feeling no concern about it.*

In our personal relationships, it may seem difficult to comprehend why someone we love and who is supposed to love us, would wilfully cause us pain or suffering.

According to the Collins dictionary, cruel as a verb means:

> *Spoil or ruin (an opportunity or a chance of success).*

When a person is on the receiving end of physical or psychological abuse, their chance for happiness and success is most definitely inhibited. Sufferers live in a state of anxiety, uncertainty and fear. Sufferers of abuse may experience diminished self-esteem, feelings of inadequacy or a lack of confidence as a result of the physical and/or psychological trauma or stress caused by their abuser. Sadly, there still seems to be a social stigma around abuse and the sufferer will often hide it from family, friends or the authorities. This allows the cycle of abuse to continue, allowing the abuser to continue and the sufferer to remain the victim.

HOW THIS RELATES TO MY STORY

I kept my abuse hidden for years from most family members and friends. To many people on the outside, our relationship was normal and we were part of a lovely family. The reason I kept my abuse secret was because:

- I felt that I was to blame in some way.

- I was ashamed.

- Each time, I believed that it was a one-off event and it wouldn't happen again.

- If everyone knew, it made it real in my own head and I didn't want to believe it was really happening.

- I thought our relationship would improve.

- I loved the father of my children and didn't want him to be punished in any way.

✒ HOW THIS RELATES TO YOUR STORY

As part of your own personal journey, I am now going to encourage you to answer some questions. Strong emotions may arise and catch you off guard, so please honour the process by giving yourself the necessary time and space to connect with your inner most thoughts and feelings. You may choose to write in a journal, rather than writing in this book as space is limited, but either way, trust and go with your gut instincts.

Q: Have you ever been ill-treated by another person? If so, how were you ill-treated? How did you feel at the time and how do you feel now?

Q: Have you ever felt emotional pain? If so, close your eyes and think of the incident, so that you can connect emotionally and describe how you felt.

Q: Has anyone ever prevented you from doing something which makes you happy? If so, why did you choose not to follow your heart? Was this a one-off incident or did/does this happen regularly?

If you feel you need some help with this, or just want to connect with me to see if you're on the right track, why not get in touch! You can *call me* on 0845 388 8130, email me at helen@evolvingyou.co.uk or simply *visit my website* **www.evolvingyou.co.uk** for more information.

We must remember that abuse isn't exclusive to personal relationships, but it can also happen in our work relationships, too. At work, abusive or bullying behaviour may be classed as:

• Persistent intimidation.

- Offensive or insulting behaviour.
- Exclusion or victimisation.
- Constant criticism.
- Humiliation.
- Misuse of power.

Sufferers of abuse at work may experience health issues as a result of the ongoing trauma caused. These may include cardiovascular problems, impaired immune system, depression and anxiety.

> *"Workplace bullying is commonly sustained by denial, ignorance and indifference, often in a climate of fear, with a common result being the premature departure of the target and reward for the perpetrator."* ~ Tim Field, Anti-Bullying Activist

People fail to report abuse at work because they:

- Don't recognise subtle abuse.
- Justify psychological abuse as 'banter'.
- Feel ashamed.
- Feel powerless.
- Are dependent on the income to survive.
- Worry about being unable to get another job.

Abuse is also present in schools, but we tend to refer to this as bullying. Despite anti-bullying campaigns, bullying is still a serious issue in many schools worldwide due to the 'code of silence' many children opt to take. Children do not report abuse due to:

- Fear of being branded a 'rat'.
- Not trusting adults to take action.
- Feeling ashamed.
- Feeling powerless.
- Fearing retaliation.

 HOW THIS RELATES TO YOUR STORY

As before, allow yourself the necessary time and space to reflect on these questions and process any feelings which arise.

Q: Have you ever been subject to intimidation at work? If so, what methods did he/she use to intimidate you? How did the persons actions make you feel?

Q: Have you ever been subject to constant criticism either at work or home? As a result of the criticism, what are your beliefs about yourself?

Q: Do you suffer from reoccurring health problems? If so, what ailments do you have.

Bullying and psychological abuse are sometimes viewed as two separate entities, when in fact they are one and the same. Schools have policies about acceptable behaviour and anti-bullying campaigns. I believe, however, that there is not enough education in schools to help children identify the more subtle forms of abuse. As children mature into their teens and then into adulthood, they are unable to recognise psychological abuse or know how to do anything about it.

Of course, in today's society, we face another form of abuse which is growing at an alarming rate. Due to the increased use of electronic digital devices and social media, children now face cyberbullying, cyberharassment and cyberstalking. In such cases, the abuser uses equipment such as mobile phones, computers or tablets to harass, torment, threaten, humiliate or embarrass their victim via text messages, chat, websites or social media sites. Examples of this are:

- Mean text messages.
- Nasty comments.
- Abusive emails.
- Rumours and gossip.
- Inappropriate pictures or videos.

Cyberbullying gives the abuser the opportunity to abuse his/her victim 24 hours a day, seven days per week, rather than just during face-to-face contact. In this type of abuse, the victim has little means of escape.

On the website nobullying.com, there is a report from the UK anti-bullying charity *Ditch the Label*. Its 2014 annual cyberbullying report which surveyed more than 10,000 youths, reported that:

- 7 in 10 young people are victims of cyberbullying.

- 37% of those are experiencing cyberbullying on a highly frequent basis.

- 20% of young people are experiencing extreme cyberbullying on a daily basis.

Andrew (Andie) Steele Smith, Australian entrepreneur and supporter of UK anti-stalking charities mentioned on his blog a survey published by the University of Bedfordshire in conjunction with the Network for Surviving Stalking, stated:

"The amount of electronic data and communication has given opportunity for areas of society to act unethically, unlawfully or immorally. One area that has given rise to great concern, and is the subject of this work, is that of cyberstalking. Figures from the Crown Prosecution Service show that during the last year, 33% of stalking incidents were by e-mail, 32% by text message and a further 8.4% were through social networking sites."

By whatever means, psychological abuse and bullying is NOT acceptable in any guise in today's society. This is because it equates to:

- ✗ Misuse.

- ✗ Exploitation.

- ✗ Manipulation.

- ✗ Taking advantage of...

- ✗ Mistreatment of...

Under the Domestic Violence, Crime and Victims Act 2004, domestic abuse is classed as a criminal offence. Sadly under this act, psychological abuse was a grey area. In August 2014, Home Secretary Theresa May launched a consultation to strengthen the law in order to provide better protection and improve police performance. In November 2014, she announced changes in the law which extended domestic violence offences to include emotional and psychological harm. Under the tough new laws, abusers could face up to fourteen years in prison for excessive controlling behaviour or emotionally abusing or threatening their partners.

On 22 November, Russell Myers reported in the Mirror:

Ms May said: *"Abuse is not just physical. Victims who are subjected to a living hell by their partners must have the confidence to come forward. I want perpetrators to be in no doubt that their cruel and controlling behaviour is criminal."*

Plaid Cymru's Elfyn Llwyd, the MP driving the new law, added: *"Coercive behaviour can be as insidious and as damaging as physical violence."*

 ## HOW THIS RELATES TO YOUR STORY

Having now spent some time reflecting upon your own story, in summary would you say that you have ever been the victim of abuse?

Q: From what you have noted so far, do you see any
      pattern occurring in the abuse you have endured or
      continue to suffer from?

Admitting to ourselves that we have been on the receiving end
of abuse can be extremely difficult. If you think you need support
to process any of the emotions which you're experiencing right
now or have *any questions* about how you're feeling, then why
not get in touch with me. If you find it easier to express your
thoughts in writing, then email me at **helen@evolvingyou.co.uk**
or, if you're ready to talk in complete confidence, then call me on
0845 388 8130.

23

The Cycle of Abuse

To aid the understanding of an abuser's behaviour and why victims stay in an abusive situation, I thought it may help to have an awareness of the abuse cycle. The *Cycle of Abuse Theory* is simplistic yet revolutionary, as it explains patterns of behaviour in an abusive relationship, as well as phases which characteristically occur before, during and after an abusive episode.

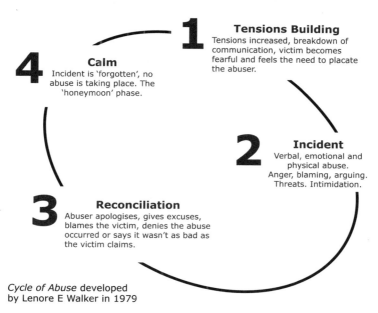

1 Tensions Building
Tensions increased, breakdown of communication, victim becomes fearful and feels the need to placate the abuser.

4 Calm
Incident is 'forgotten', no abuse is taking place. The 'honeymoon' phase.

2 Incident
Verbal, emotional and physical abuse. Anger, blaming, arguing. Threats. Intimidation.

3 Reconciliation
Abuser apologises, gives excuses, blames the victim, denies the abuse occurred or says it wasn't as bad as the victim claims.

Cycle of Abuse developed by Lenore E Walker in 1979

Critics have argued that the theory may be flawed as it cannot be universally applied to all cases of abuse. All relationships are unique and abuse is inconsistent, so therefore individual experiences will vary. For example, the length of time spent in each phase of the cycle may vary from minutes to months or may even be omitted completely in some cases. I have chosen to include this, however, to provide insight into possible cycles of behaviour. This may help you recognise if this applies to any of your past or current relationships and help you with the questions on the following pages.

1. TENSION BUILDING

Stress is a huge issue in today's society and we face the growing pressures on a day-to-day basis. In basic terms, stress is the reaction that we experience to situations which overwhelm us or create feelings of being unable to cope. Stress is subjective, as what creates stress in one person may motivate another, depending on their personality type.

Stressors are things which cause a stress response, and again they are personal to an individual. Stressors may be physical or psychological and they include:

- Money concerns
- Relationship issues
- Work demands
- Redundancy
- Life changes
- Moving house
- Death of a family member or friend
- Conflict over children
- Illness

When we experience stress, the body will release adrenaline, causing the heart rate to increase and glucose to be released for added energy. This is known as the fight or flight response - its an adaptive response which has remained with us through evolution. During this phase of the abuse cycle, both the abuser and the sufferer will be in stress but for different reasons. In my opinion, stress can often play a part in this section of the cycle however it is NOT an excuse to justify the behaviour. Would teaching stress management in schools help to reduce the number of abuse cases in the future, I wonder?

Predominantly, this period of the cycle involves:

- Tension starts and steadily builds.

- Abuser may feel ignored, threatened or annoyed.

- Communication breaks down and abuser may give sufferer the silent treatment.

- Victim feels the need to dissolve the situation.

- Interpersonal tension rises, with possible name calling, shouting and swearing.

- Victim feels uneasy and as if 'treading on eggshells'.

During this phase the abuser may demonstrate the following behaviours;

- Jealousy and invalidation
- Insults and/or sarcasm
- Threats and accusations
- Control
- Mood swings

2. INCIDENT or ACTING OUT

Abuse here can take many forms. In cases of physical abuse, the abuser would:

- Inflict physical pain and/or injury.

- Constrain the sufferer to prevent them leaving.

- Throwing things.

In cases of psychological abuse, the 'acting out' stage may last longer as the abuser may repeatedly trick the sufferer into distrusting his/her own memory, perceptions and judgement. It involves:

- Withholding – refusing to listen, or share emotions.

- Countering – creating uncertainty.

- Blocking – changing of conversation to question sufferers thoughts.

- Trivialising – making sufferer believe his/her needs aren't important.

- Forgetting/denial – abuser pretends to forget things that are important to the sufferer.

- Projection – abuser puts responsibility of his/her feelings onto sufferer.

- Accusing/blaming – abuser blames victim for his/her act.

- Generalisation – abuser exaggerates small truths.

- Domination – abuser controls what the sufferer does.

- Humiliation – abuser publically puts down sufferer.

- Justification - abuser uses jealousy to justify his/her actions.

- Judgment – abuser makes a judgement about the sufferer, so the sufferer does what is necessary to please.

- Manipulation – abuser gains control over sufferer.

In some cases, the abuser will use both physical and psychological abuse, but whatever the chosen method, the abuser is always trying to gain control and hold the power in the relationship.

3. RECONCILIATION

This part will be different, depending upon the type of incident.

In physical abuse cases, the abuser may:

- Feel remorseful.

- Show sorrow.

- Experience guilt.

In psychological abuse cases, the abuser may:

- Walk away with little or no comment.

- Be unaware of doing anything wrong.

Reconciliation may be characterised by:

- An apology.

- Begging for forgiveness.

- Promising that it won't happen again.

- Promising change.

- Affection/make up sex.

- Minimising or denying the abuse.

- Blaming the victim for the abuse.

- Threatening suicide to prevent the victim from leaving.

The abuser is always very convincing during the reconciliation phase, so that the sufferer will stay and the cycle can continue. The sufferer may believe that the relationship isn't all that bad after all, and make excuses to justify the abuser's behaviour.

4. CALM

I see this as the 'life back to normal' phase. During this stage, normal life is resumed to some degree and the abuse slows or stops completely. The abuser acts as if the abuse never happened and it gets successfully brushed under the carpet whilst the sufferer believes that the abuse has stopped. The abuser may:

- Give gifts to the sufferer.

- Take the sufferer out.

- Temporarily keep promises.

- Improve communication.

- Be more attentive and spend time with sufferer and/or family.

- Help with housework/chores.

- Give compliments.

Underlying issues that are not properly addressed and dealt with physically, emotionally and mentally and that are unresolved, simply fuel the cycle further. The cycle continues and therefore tension will begin to build and lead to stage one again.

HOW THIS RELATES TO YOUR STORY

Tension

Q: Have you experienced periods of tension in your past or current relationship? If so, what are the signs? How do you feel when this happens?

Incident

Q: In your past or current relationship, did/does your partner: (Tick all that apply.)

☐ Refuse to listen to you.

☐ Create uncertainty around an event.

☐ Change the conversation so that you question your own thoughts/ feelings.

☐ Lead you to believe that your thoughts and feelings are unimportant.

☐ Pretend to forget things which are important to you.

☐ Blame you for what he/she has done.

☐ Exaggerate small truths or repeatedly tell lies.

☐ Control what you do, with whom and when.

☐ Put you down in front of family, friends and/or in public.

☐ Use jealousy as a reason for his/her actions.

☐ Use manipulation and/or control to get his/her own way.

Reconciliation

Q: Following an incident, did/does your partner: (Tick all that apply.)

☐ Show remorse?

☐ Walk away and refuse to discuss anything further?

☐ Apologise?

☐ Beg for forgiveness?

☐ Promise it won't happen again?

☐ Promise to change?

☐ Become increasingly affectionate?

☐ Minimise or deny what happened?

Calm

Q: **Past Relationships**: In general, how did your partner behave towards you in everyday life?

Q: **Current relationship**: How does your partner behave towards you, the majority of the time?

24
Karma

What goes around, comes around.

What is Karma?

To understand karmic relationships, we first have to understand *The Law of Karma*. Karma in Sanskrit means action, work or deed, and in both Buddhism and Hinduism, it is the sum of a person's deed in this and past states of existence, that decides their current and future fate. Good intent and deed contributes to good karma, whereas bad intent and deed contributes to bad karma. Karma ensures that as individuals, we all have the opportunity to 'take turns' in being both the giver and receiver, so that we can fully appreciate and integrate the rewards or consequences of our actions.

My Karmic Awakening

Before I explain karmic relationships, I would first like to share with you my own personal story, which happened in 2005, when Drew was just three years old. I call this my *karmic awakening,* as before this time, I was unaware of the true meaning of karma and had no conscious thoughts or beliefs about past lives.

Drew and I were happily playing in his bedroom one day when

he turned to me and said, *"I am so happy that I chose you to be my mummy."*

I didn't fully comprehend what Drew was saying, but gratefully replied, *"I am happy that you chose me too darling."*

Drew then said, *"when I was with God, I looked down and said that I wanted you to be my mummy."*

Drew's words shocked me, as we aren't a religious family, so I was unsure where he had heard about God and knew that people refer to heaven as looking down on us.

The following day, I started researching past lives, as Drew had ignited my curiosity and I wanted to understand properly what he had talked about. Following my research, I decided to book an appointment with a past life regression therapist, so that I could understand more about past lives and the effect they have on our current life. I had no specific expectations and went with a fully open mind about what I may experience and whether it would be successful or not. To my surprise, I was able to regress easily and I was soon reliving a life that my soul had experienced during the middle ages. I was an adolescent girl who lived in a small castle-like home with just my father, as my mother had passed away during child birth.

I was astonished at the clarity of my visions and emotional experiences - it was as if I was genuinely back living my life as that character. I noticed very early on in the regression that I felt intensely repressed by my father and his behaviour. He was exceedingly controlling, resulting in me feeling powerless and subservient to his needs. My father had high expectations of me and would dictate what I could do, with whom and when. His treatment was suffocating and restricted my personality, creativity and ability to be my true self.

In order to tolerate such control, I regularly sought reprieve in a local village community, which I journeyed to on horseback.

The village was located near the woods and my time there was a stark contrast to life at home with my father. The villagers accepted me for who I was, encouraged my individuality and gave me a feeling of freedom. To cut a long story short, as I grew up my father struggled to retain his control over me and so ordered me to be burnt at the stake as a witch. In my death, I was finally free of his control and power, or so I thought.

I was encouraged by the therapist to draw direct comparisons between my life then and my current life and I quickly realised that my father in my past life was Robert. In my past life, death temporarily set me free from his control, but the karmic bond that we shared meant that we would reincarnate together in this lifetime. In every lifetime, we are offered the chance for soul freedom, which means consciously evolving beyond our restrictions and limitations.

Since my past life regression, I have continued to feed my hunger for knowledge and now fully understand that the lessons I have experienced in this lifetime, include:

- Being able to recognise psychological abuse.
- How to cut etheric cords.
- Evolving beyond victim consciousness.
- Connecting with my own personal power.
- Living an authentic life by my core values.
- Becoming the creator of my own life and destiny.
- Using my experiences to help others do the same.

During every incarnation, we are given the gift of free will, so in my opinion we have three choices:

- Be a sufferer (victim).

- Be an abuser (persecutor).

- Be (self-realised)

I am exceptionally grateful to Drew for the conversation we had that day, as he truly helped me to resolve and evolve beyond my karmic bonds. Sadly, we are unable to free ourselves of these toxic bonds in an instant. Realisation or acknowledgment is just the first step in the process, which then needs to be followed with inner healing work. The inner journey work I have successfully completed has enabled me to heal my wounds from this and other lifetimes, and it was my motivation to help others do the same. As a Past Life Regression Therapist myself now, as well as a Transpersonal Hypnotherapist and Seichem Reiki Master and Teacher, I believe inner journey healing and transpersonal work is an exceedingly powerful healing tool.

✒ HOW THIS RELATES TO YOUR STORY

Q: Do you believe in karma? Why?

Q: Do you believe in past lives?

Q: Have you ever experienced past life connections when:

☐   Visiting somewhere and having a Déjà vu moment?

☐   When meeting someone for the first time but who feels familiar?

☐   Experiencing a vivid dream which felt exceptionally real?

25
Relationships

Karmic Relationships

Every relationship we enter into, is karmic in nature on some level. Our past life experiences provide our soul with a kaleidoscope of experiences and as a result, when we meet a person in this lifetime, we are not consciously aware whether our connection will be a good or bad one. When we meet someone, we simply know whether we are drawn to them or not. We could refer to this as the Karmic Magnet.

What is a Karmic Relationship?

Some karmic relationships are positive so may be considered soulmate relationships. These types of relationships are supportive and aid our soul's evolution in becoming 'whole' and self-realised.

Other relationships may be negative, with a powerful, toxic compulsion. These can be classed as woundmate relationships. This destructive type of relationship locks us in unhealthy cycles which deepen our wounds further. These connections are never meant to be lasting ones, due to their nature, as most will involve some level of psychological abuse. It is their compelling and addictive nature that entraps us in continuous voyages around the abuse cycle. Each lifetime, however, offers a new chance to start afresh and change the events of past ones.

How to recognise a negative karmic relationship:

- Abuse
- Addictions
- Anger or rage
- Arguments
- Restrictions
- Jealousy
- Selfishness
- Regular break-ups

Negative karmic relationships provide us with two choices:

1. Change nothing

If we choose not to acknowledge what is happening and therefore change nothing, a woundmate relationship will only deepen our wounds and bring us more of the same through the Law of Attraction.

2. Change everything

If we choose to open our eyes, woundmate relationships offer ideal opportunities to heal our wounds, by undertaking the necessary inner journey work. Inner healing is the most precious gift that we can offer ourselves, as it enables us to live a life free from fear and restrictions.

When we view our relationships in terms of their karma, I believe that we are able to detach ourselves emotionally, see the bigger picture and make mind-heart-gut decisions. We begin to understand what lesson(s) that relationship offers, so that karma can be resolved and brought back into balance. Knowledge provides us with information and understanding, but we need to take action to break the karmic bond so that we do not attract a similar relationship through the Law of Attraction. For this, inner healing is necessary.

HOW THIS RELATES TO MY STORY

Following my past life regression session, I realised that my relationship with Robert was a karmic one, which was why I was compelled to give him repeated chances time and time again. My relationship with Robert caused fear, anxiety and sadness. Since our divorce, I still have to have contact with Robert as he is the father of our children. However, through inner journey work I have successfully released the karmic bond between us and healed my wounds, which enables me to view our relationship differently. We don't have to physically be in a relationship with someone for them to continue their pattern of behaviour and psychological abuse. Whilst I have changed, Robert has chosen to stay the same. However, as I am consciously aware of his strategies of abuse, I remain detached and his attempts to drag me back into the abuse cycle no longer work. If existing strategies have no affect, an abuser will try to find other means of regaining control and power, for example via the children. Robert continues to offer me chances to put into practice what I have learnt over the years and 'walk my talk', so he is a great teacher.

✒ HOW THIS RELATES TO YOUR STORY

Q: Please indicate if you have ever experienced a relationship
    with a family member, friend or partner which was:
    (Tick all that apply.)

☐ Destructive

☐ Compelling/ addictive

☐ Involved mind games

☐ Emotionally toxic

☐ Involved jealousy

☐ Abusive

☐ Predominantly one-way

☐ Argumentative

☐ On one day and off the next

☐ Fear driven

☐ Based mainly on pleasing the other person

☐ Caused inadequacy

☐ Adversely effected your self-esteem

Q: How do you feel when you see that particular person?
    Are you yourself or do you adapt your behaviour? Why?

Soulmate Relationship

What is a soulmate?

In its simplest terms, a soulmate is a resolved karmic relationship. For example, an obligation that has been fulfilled, a conflict that has been resolved or a deed that has been forgiven.

"A soulmate is someone who has locks that fit our keys, and keys to fit our locks." ~ Richard Bach, American author

---

What is a soulmate relationship?

A soulmate relationship is life-changing, as it's founded on compromise and unity, so very different from a power struggle woundmate relationship. Soulmate relationships are instantly recognisable by their natural affinity, deep level of comfort and the safety they provide. Our soulmate enables us to feel secure, fully healed and whole, so that no piece of our jigsaw is missing. When we are 'whole', we can live life authentically, from a place of real love and mutual respect.

A soulmate relationship may still have certain areas to be refined but partners will experience an inner knowing that these issues

can and will be resolved together. This type of relationship is healthy and grows as we do.

How to recognise a soulmate relationship:

- Unconditional love.
- Mutual respect.
- Feel secure and protected.
- Strong mental connection – minds in tune.
- Share a fundamental bond.
- Instant trust that you both share.
- Possess matching significant life values.
- Readily resolve problems as they arise.
- Inner cognition that you've known each other before.
- Beautiful, peaceful and joyful experience.
- Patience and encouragement.
- Equality.
- Space to grow.

I trust this information is useful and will enable you to recognise which of your past and current family, friends and work colleague relationships are woundmate and which are soulmates. If you are still looking for your 'love' soulmate, then I trust this information will aid your journey in making the right choice for you.

'LOOKING FOR LOVE' CLIENT STUDY:

A female client recently came to me for help in looking for her Mr Right. After successfully completing inner journey work together on her career, she was now ready to focus her attention on her personal life. On a conscious level, she believed that she was ready to meet the man of her dreams and so struggled to understand why she was so 'unlucky in love'. Through our collaboration during an inner journey session, my client realised that she still had etheric cords to her past boyfriends, as well as unresolved negative thoughts and feelings towards them. Unconsciously, she was contaminating her own energy, which in turn was preventing her from achieving what she really wanted.

During the session, we worked together using various techniques to heal her mental and emotional wounds from her experiences with her past boyfriends, and released the toxic energy that she was unconsciously holding on to. My client was then able to identify for herself the lessons that she had gained from each relationship and how they had helped her grow as a human and spiritual soul. Her past boyfriends were woundmates in her quest to becoming 'whole'. By gifting herself the opportunity to inner journey and heal her wounds, she had also provided herself with the opportunity to meet her soulmate. One of the Laws of the Universe is the Law of Attraction - *'like attracts like'* - and by holding on to low vibrational energies such as heartbreak, anger or fear, my client was unknowingly attracting more boyfriends of the same character. By healing her wounds and releasing these dense energy blocks, my client had raised her vibration, enabling her to attract a higher vibrational mate.

✎ HOW THIS RELATES TO YOUR STORY

Q: Please indicate if you have ever experienced a relationship
     with a family member, friend or partner which was:
     (Tick all that apply.)

☐   Loving

☐   Supportive

☐   Based on compromise

☐   Mutually respectful

☐   Equal

☐   Comfortable

☐   Safe and secure

☐   Trustworthy

☐   Encouraging

☐   Compassionate

☐   Forgiving

☐   Joyful

List the people in which you share a 'soulmate' relationship.
*Feel blessed to have been gifted with these relationships and
maybe give thanks in some way in acknowledgement of these
people.*

Woundmate Relationship

What is a woundmate?

A woundmate is the coming together of two souls with unresolved emotional issues/patterns, or who mirror each other's wounds. In this type of relationship, wounds will be triggered with three possible outcomes:

Outcome One

Both parties take personal responsibility for their own inner journey in order to transform their wounds. By successfully healing their wounds, they are able to progress beyond them, unite, become soulmates and live a happy life.

Outcome Two

One person takes personal responsibility for their wounds and successfully transforms them in order to progress the relationship. The other party refuses to acknowledge or take responsibility, furthering the divide in the relationship. This relationship experiences continuous challenges, or may be brought to an end as the divide grows.

Outcome Three

Nobody is willing to take personal responsibility for their own inner journey, resulting in unhealed wounds and both parties continuously living in a cycle of unhealthy patterns of behaviour. Inevitably, this relationship will come to an end at some point.

HOW THIS RELATES TO MY STORY

Robert was a woundmate who triggered my past wounds from this and other lifetimes, and, who through his words and actions, made them even deeper. I was happy to take responsibility for my part and heal my wounds, but Robert would not take responsibility for his part in our relationship or see any wrong in his behaviour. Therefore, over the years, the divide between us grew and therefore the only outcome - in my opinion - was for us to separate.

A person has to want to change. We cannot make someone change, otherwise we become manipulative in the process. As the saying states:

"You can lead a horse to water but you can't make it drink."

Some clients come to me wanting to change their partners, but I often recite the Aldous Huxley quote to them, which is mentioned earlier:

"I wanted to change the world. But I have found that the only thing one can be sure of changing is oneself."
~ Aldous Huxley

Or the serenity prayer:

"God, grant me the serenity to accept
the things I cannot change,
The courage to change the things I can,
And the wisdom to know the difference."

 HOW THIS RELATES TO YOUR STORY

Q: Make a list of people who you have shared a 'wound-mate' relationship with. This can include all aspects of your life, from school, work, family, friends and partners.

Q: Are you currently experiencing a woundmate relationship? If so, how does the relationship make you feel?

Q: What steps could you take to change this relationship?

When in the midst of a woundmate relationship, it sometimes can be difficult to see the wood for the trees due to its emotional and unsettling nature. We may self-sabotage in changing our life for the better, through fear, uncertainty or not wanting to confront reality. If you feel that you are struggling to answer the above questions, or unsure how to take the necessary steps for change, then be assured we can find an appropriate solution for you. Every person and each relationship is unique, which is why during one-to-one sessions we can easily and readily ascertain a Self-Realisation plan for you to work with. If you would like further information, why not speak to me direct by booking a **FREE initial chat** on where you're at and if indeed I can help you. Simply call on 0845 388 8130 and I look forward to hearing from you.

26
Wounds

What are wounds?

When I refer to wounds in this book, I am not referring to physical wounds but psychological ones. In my experience, psychological wounds are thoughts and/or emotions from our experiences in this or other lifetimes, which may have been repressed, ignored or denied at the time of the experience.

Mental wounds

From birth, we develop mental wounds from the information we see, hear or experience. These thoughts get stored in our subconscious mind, which is unable to differentiate right from wrong, good from bad or reality from imagination. It has no reasoning skills to judge the information it receives, and so messages are taken as true fact and form our belief system. Examples of mental wounds that affect our mind and thinking are thoughts of:

- Self-confidence – e.g. I am not good enough.

- Self-blame – e.g. everything is my fault.

- Self-doubt – e.g. I must be a bad person.

- Self-esteem – e.g. I am not worthy.

- Self-criticism – e.g. I could do better.

Emotional wounds

Our emotions are just as real and can be as painful as physical pain. Emotional wounds develop from how we feel about someone or something, as well as from unexpressed or swallowed feelings. These most commonly affect our heart and can be feelings of:

- Hurt
- Fear
- Rage or anger
- Panic
- Helplessness
- Grief
- Resentment
- Guilt
- Shame
- Absence of forgiveness

Psychological wounds

These wounds are generally held in our stomach and challenge our natural gut instinct and/or intuition. These wounds include:

- Fear
- Doubt
- Anxiety
- Questioning our own judgement

Throughout our lifetime, if we suppress, ignore or deny our thoughts, feelings or instincts, or have them repressed, ignored or denied by others, then deep wounds are formed. These unconscious wounds continue to damage the present decisions and actions we take in life, inhibiting our success and happiness. If these wounds go unhealed, the previous chapters in our life story control the creation of new future chapters, restricting the growth of our creative and true self. We cannot change our past experiences, but the great news is that we can change how we think or feel about them.

During my extensive work with clients, I discovered the key to the lasting transformation of a person's wounds. Using regression techniques, combined with various healing methods, I facilitated sessions where clients were able to identify and successfully transform their own limiting thoughts and suppressed feelings. This ensured that they released limiting beliefs and patterns of behaviour, which were not in alignment with their own core values, and formed new thoughts and feelings which were congruent and in alignment with their authentic self. Clients were no longer a prisoner of their story, but free to create a new chapter in their lives.

 ## HOW THIS RELATES TO YOUR STORY

In the next set of statements, it's really important that you are completely honest with yourself. I would suggest placing one hand on your heart and the other on your stomach, as you say the statements out loud and then intuitively write down the first number which comes to mind. Do not change your score, as your first response is the most intuitive, whereas your second response may be coming from the ego. Also, take notice which statements evoke particularly strong emotions within you, and mark a star by them. At the end of the exercise, go back to the starred statements and explore how long you have felt that way. Is this an old or new belief about your 'self'? On a scale of 1 – 10 (1= disagree and 10 = wholly agree), rate the following:

Set One

Self-belief – I can achieve whatever I desire in life.

Self-confidence – I trust and know that I am good enough.

Self-control – I am in control of my thoughts and feelings.

Self-determination – I am able to make decisions for myself without outside influences.

Self-discipline – I am able to control my desires and behaviour at all times.

Self-esteem – I am worthy of all life has to offer me.

Self-expression – I confidently express my personality and feelings without fear of judgement.

Self-image – I value myself and know my true worth.

Self-love – I love myself unconditionally.

Self-respect – I am proud of myself and my abilities.

Set Two

Self-blame – Everything which goes wrong is my fault.

Self-criticism – I can't do things as well as others and whatever I do, its never good enough.

Self-conscious – I get embarrassed easily.

Self-doubt – I have little faith in myself and my abilities.

Self-defence – I feel that I have to defend myself from the opinions of others.

Self-less – I put others before myself.

Self-pity – I often pity and feel sorry myself.

Self-sacrifice – I put the needs of others before myself.

What do you notice about your scores in each set of statements? Are your scores of 8, 9 and 10 mainly in set one, or set two? If your higher scores are in set one, then I predict that you have already undertaken some form of personal development. If you notice any scores in this area which are 8 or below, then I would suggest that these are areas you may like to investigate further.

If your higher scores are in set two, you may be carrying wounds from your past which require attention and healing. Your life up until this moment has shaped the person you are today, and your interaction with others will have contributed towards your inner belief system, either in a positive, negative or neutral manner. The *great news* is that your belief system, just like computer software, can be *updated* at any time you wish. The even *better news* is that **TODAY,** you can take the next step in changing your S.E.L.F (Soul Evolution to Life Freedom) by either engaging with me via email, on **helen@evolvingyou.co.uk**, in a one-to-one session, via my online programs or attending a seminar. Simply go to **www.evolvingyou.co.uk** for more information about the services I offer.

27
Cord Connections

Invisible energy cords, which are like umbilical cords, exist between people, objects, places and events. These cords are sometimes referred to as etheric cords and can be seen through the mind's eye or psychic eye. Energy flows back and forth through these cords. New cords are created whenever we:

- Form a relationship with someone.

- Connect with an object.

- Visit a place.

- Experience an incident/event.

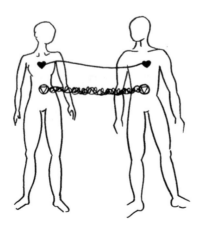

The longer the relationship, or the more interactions we have with a person, object, place or event, the greater the number and thickness of these cords.

The cords that connect us change and grow in line with the relationship, and so the nature of the cord represents the nature of the relationship. We have:

- Genetic cords to our parents and ancestral line.
- Relational cords to other people.

Healthy Cords

- Bright in colour.
- Flexible for freedom.
- Facilitate free will.
- Allow transition.

Unhealthy Cords

- Dark, heavy, stiff and brittle in nature.
- Cause habitual interaction.
- Allow others to drain our energy.
- Resist personal growth and change.

Some therapists believe in cutting negative or unhealthy cords on behalf of the client. However, in my experience, this is not best practice for the client and may cause trauma and/or cords to re-attach over time. Etheric cords hold a person's thoughts and feelings, so if the client has not acknowledged, healed and released any negative beliefs or emotions from that cord, it can bring about other challenges for the client.

CLIENT STUDY – CUTTING THE CORDS FOLLOWING DIVORCE

A client came to see me for help, as she had been divorced for many years but was struggling to move on from her abusive relationship. She recognised that her ex-husband had treated her badly, but somehow she just couldn't let him go. He still consumed her mind and heart.

Together, we completed some inner journey work to heal the cords which still tied them together. It became apparent that my client still held the belief that she was to blame in some way, or that she wasn't good enough for him. These mental and emotional wounds were strengthening the cords between them and keeping the client in victim consciousness.

During the session, the client realised that they shared a karmic relationship and could readily see the lessons that the relationship provided. With this insight, her wounds were then easier to heal using various healing tools and techniques. Once the wounds were healed, the cords changed and were ready to be cut. The client was then free to transform her negative cycles and patterns of behaviour, so that she could go on to meet her soulmate.

HOW THIS RELATES TO YOUR STORY

Q: Refer back to your wound-mate list. It's highly likely that you still have energy cords to these people. Close your eyes and think of each person on your list in turn. Notice your emotional responses when you think about each person and write down your feelings.

28
The Law of Attraction

There are twelve universal laws and the *Law of Attraction* is just one of them. You don't have to believe in this law for it to have an effect every minute of every day of your life. For example, you don't have to believe in the Law of Gravity for gravity to work, do you?

In simple terms, the *Law of Attraction* means 'like attracts like,' so teachers of this philosophy believe that focusing on:

- Positive thoughts bring about positive results.

- Negative thoughts bring about negative results.

When many people talk of this law they use the phrase:

"Ask. Believe. Receive."

In my experience, using the *Law of Attraction* is not that simple, as we are made of energy and therefore have to take into account the energy of our inner reality. Simply identifying what we want - asking for it on a goal chart or map and then believing it will come true - does not help us to get what we want if our energy is not congruent with what we are asking for.

Let's take an easy example, say a new car. If a person chooses a new car, sits in it, takes it on a test drive and then puts an image of the car on their dream board, do you think the person will get a new car?

In some cases, maybe, but in the majority I would suspect not. In my experience, the *Law of Attraction* does not solely work in this way. Let's look at the person identified above as wanting a new car. If this person is carrying a mental pattern of unworthiness, or has an emotional block of not being good enough, then the *Law of Attraction* will restrict them in co-creating a new car until they have dealt with their inner reality and changed their energy.

By changing our inner reality to transform negative mental patterns, and emotional restrictions, we resolve karma and/or release cords, and in return our energy vibration is raised. This powerful force can then work with us in co-creating a new reality in relation to our relationship, career, health and wealth, assisting us to return to our authentic, limitless self and become self-realised.

HOW THIS RELATES TO MY STORY

Initially, I gained much knowledge about psychological abuse, abuser strategies, karma and energy cords, but knowledge alone could not change my relationship with Robert. This was because I was carrying low vibrational energy of:

- Victim Consciousness
- Fear
- Anger
- Restriction
- Doubt

The *Law of Attraction*, therefore, brought me more of the same as like attracts like. I manifested more situations to be a victim, to be controlled, and feel fearful and unworthy. Hence, I continued to suffer in my relationship with Robert, as well as in certain friendships, at work and in my experiences with two Reiki masters.

By transforming my inner reality to heal the stories behind the low vibrational energies I was carrying, I raised my vibrational energy to:

- Be balanced, grounded and centred.
- Live authentically.
- Connect with my whole self and inner power.
- Live in line with my core values.

Therefore, the *Law of Attraction* brought me new positive circumstances, as like attracts like. I find it easier and quicker to co-create from a healed mind and body than from a wounded one.

 ## HOW THIS RELATES TO YOUR STORY

Q: Write a list of things which you would like to achieve in life but have been struggling to. Ask yourself "*What aspect of me is blocking this?*" Maybe refer back to your notes on page 186 to discover what beliefs may be blocking your dreams.

Q: What steps could you take to transform these negative
     restrictions?

If you feel you need some help with this, or just want to
connect with me to see if you're on the right track, why not get
in touch! You can call me on 0845 388 8130, email me at
helen@evolvingyou.co.uk   or   simply   visit   my   website
www.evolvingyou.co.uk for more information.

29
Victim Consciousness

Unhealed wounds and/or negative cords can keep a person locked in victim consciousness, which is primarily a learned personality trait. When a person enters into a dysfunctional relationship, they remain in victimhood and continue to deny their own abilities and personal power, putting the other person above themselves. Their core belief may be that there is something wrong with them, especially in the case of psychological abuse. Others may believe that the outside world is responsible for the abuse they suffer, and that they are powerless to do anything about their life.

Vulnerable people are easier to emotionally and psychologically manipulate, so they therefore make an ideal victim for an abuser. Low levels of self-worth and/or self-esteem means that they will seek approval and acceptance from other people, especially in an intimate relationship. Taking care of others fulfils a deep need within them to feel useful and loved. I say these words from experience, as at eighteen years of age, I was a vulnerable person.

Manipulation itself is a powerful tool and a means of control and power. Methods of gaining control can be devious, covert or overt and/or involve pure domination. Manipulators like to keep their victims in a constant state of uncertainty by giving double messages building a person up then cutting them down, being wounding in their communication and projecting their own feelings on to them. In my lifetime, I have experienced and witnessed all of these methods first-hand in my relationships, friendships, and at work.

HOW THIS RELATES TO MY STORY

Robert had mastered his well-rehearsed formula to cleverly uncover and gauge a woman's Achilles' heel, which once exposed, could be used for his own personal gain. He would get to know a woman first by simply talking to her about herself. He would come across as a good listener, who was genuinely interested in learning all about her life, including her hopes, dreams and fears, as well any hurt she had experienced. It is no coincidence that most of his victims had been cheated on by past boyfriends. When hearing this news, he would appear shocked to learn of the boyfriend's infidelity and would express his surprise as to why a man would cheat on such a wonderful, loving, caring and beautiful woman.

At the right moment, Robert would share his own sob story to guarantee that he got the sympathy vote. The version I was told involved an ex-girlfriend leaving him for a Manchester United and England footballer. I am unsure of the story he uses today. Once on the hook, the abuser, like a predator, can successfully manipulate his prey. In Robert's case, he would pretend to have the woman's best interests at heart, and would come across as being emotionally sensitive and interested. He would have a laugh, show himself as vulnerable yet strong, whilst all the time knowing the correct words to use. It had become nothing more than a script that Robert could perform to different women for his own entertainment. If a woman was not receptive to his manipulation, Robert could swiftly move on to the next target.

A person with victim mentality will think, speak and behave as a victim, as he/she has bought into the belief that they are one, which ultimately prevents them from experiencing true freedom.

A victim may:

- Think and believe that something or someone else is responsible for their experiences.
- Allow something or someone else to control them.
- Feel powerless about what happens to them.
- Feel continuously wronged.

"No one can make you feel inferior without your consent."
~ *Eleanor Roosevelt*

I allowed myself to remain a victim for many years, believing that I was helpless to do anything about it. In reality though, it is the victim who holds the power and is the one who can make the abuse stop. Once I realised that I had the power to evolve beyond victim consciousness and do the necessary inner journey work to heal my wounds and connect to my personal power, I had the strength to leave.

The key to transcending victim consciousness is:

- Strong desire to change.
- Recognition of being in victim state.
- Awareness of mental and emotional patterning.
- Healing of wounds.
- Healing and cutting of cords.
- Application of positive tools to change habitual behaviour.
- Living authentically by personal core values.

✎ <u>HOW THIS RELATES TO YOUR STORY</u>

Q: List the problems that you have experienced in life;

Q: On a scale of 1 – 10 (10 being highest) please rate the
      following statements:

☐   How strong is your desire to change?

☐   How much would you like to heal your wounds?

☐   What level of responsibility are you willing to take for
      your life?

☐   Are you willing to learn new tools to change habitual
      thoughts and behaviours?

☐   Are you ready to take action today?

Q: Who can change your life?*

---

*The answer to the last question is 'Me' - if you wrote anything
else, then I suggest you get in touch! Why not call me on 0845
388 8130 or email me at helen@evolvingyou.co.uk and take your
first step to self-realisation.

A Final Word From The Author

"Our deepest fear is not that we are inadequate. Our deepest fear is that we are powerful beyond measure. It is our light, not our darkness that most frightens us. We ask ourselves, Who am I to be brilliant, gorgeous, talented, fabulous? Actually, who are you not to be?"
Marianne Williamson

It's easy to go through life with our head buried firmly in the sand. I should know, I did it for many years. However, sooner or later we will suffocate, so we need to raise our head out of the sand and breathe. When our head is out of the dark sand and in the sunshine, we have the ability to face the reality of our life. I struggled to do this for many years, with my head regularly moving in and out of the sand, as I felt a failure and was too scared to see what my life had become.

Keeping my head out of the sand was easier than I initially thought. For years, I punished myself mentally and emotionally, wondering what was wrong with me. However, I realised that there was nothing wrong with me but there was something wrong with my relationship. My partner and I were not compatible. That's not to say I am perfect. In fact, through inner journey work I had to be honest with myself, look myself in the mirror and see my imperfections and be honest about my wounds.

By steadily working through my wounds, I made small changes and gradually became more and more empowered.

That isn't to say that I have healed all of my wounds, as new experiences will always bring new challenges and highlight new wounds to be healed. I am not perfect but I have learnt to love my imperfections, so I now believe that:

- ✓ I am good enough.

- ✓ I am worthy.

- ✓ I honour my core values.

- ✓ I am happy to be an individual.

- ✓ I embrace my creativity.

- ✓ I deserve love.

I wish you well on your life journey and trust that you find your power and worth.

Best wishes and magical blessings,

Helen

How I Can Help You

Many suffer in silence, not wanting to share their inner most thoughts and feelings with friends or family, through fear of judgement or criticism. This is completely normal. Some are comfortable seeking help from a professional, whilst others don't know what help is available to them, who to go to, or what will benefit them in the short and long-term.

I have experienced first-hand psychological abuse, anxiety attacks and adrenal fatigue, as well as divorce, bereavement, redundancy, plus many more life challenges. I have successfully overcome them to transform my life, to rid myself of fear and desperation, and experience happiness and joy. That's what I would like for you; as happiness is our birth-right.

I have committed years of time and investment in perfecting the most appropriate tools and techniques to enable people to break free from limiting beliefs and negative habitual behaviours so that they can become truly self-realised. Therefore, you have the benefit of my extensive knowledge, experience and expertise. You don't have to suffer in silence anymore; I am *here* to help you.

Do you feel any of these…

- Dissatisfied with some aspects of your life?

- Feelings of being helpless?

- Fearful/ anxious/ worried as though life controls you rather than you controlling it?

- You've got into bad habits that are causing your thoughts to be predominantly negative?

- You've listened to advice of others rather than connecting with and trusting your gut instinct?

If you have answered yes to any of these, then it's decision time! *You can do one of three things...*

1. Put this book down and do **nothing**. However, remember Albert Einstein's definition of insanity is *'Doing the same thing over and over again and expecting different results'*. Therefore, what changes do you expect to happen if you do nothing?

2. You can go forward on your own, which involves trial and error, a lot of time and the use of techniques which may or may not work for you.

3. Engage with me, a professional in my field, so that together we can identify your blocks, change habitual behaviour and transform limiting beliefs so that you become self-realised. In the process you will create a freedom based-life; freedom from fear, judgement, self-criticism, worry and anxiety. This is your ticket to freedom. *Will you take it?*

The best investment you can make is self-investment, so get in contact with me today by whatever means you are comfortable with. If you feel ready to chat, then dial 0845 388 8130 and talk to me directly so that we can discuss where you are right now, what you want to achieve and how we can work together to move you from a place of self-limitation to self- realisation. If I believe we are a good fit, then we'll talk about how we can work together. But if I believe I can't, then I will point you in the right direction. If you're a little nervous, about talking to me directly, then send an email to me instead to **helen@evolvingyou.co.uk.** If you're unsure what services best match your needs, then go to my website for more information about what I offer at: **www.evolvingyou.co.uk.**

What Clients Have Said About Working With Helen

I have had several sessions with Helen and her approach is very natural and non-invasive. She is supportive and challenging and comes from a place of unconditional love. What I really love is how she creates the space and asks the right questions for you to go on a journey and get your own answers, which to me is the most empowering type of healing you can receive. This, combined with her intuition, insights, reiki skills and chakra balancing, makes Helen a first choice for me and I have been to many healers over the years.

Jo Simpson ~ *Leadership Alignment & Author*

Helen is in a league of her own as a Self-Realisation healer and mentor. She is gentle and kind but more importantly non-judgemental. Helen provides clients with empowering tools and techniques, as she believes the only person who can fix themselves, is themselves – which is right! Helen lives by her own advice and walks her talk, but doesn't tell her clients what to do, but instead helps them make their own decisions and choose the right path for themselves. Helen has been in my life for many years now and in 2014, she supported me through what was a very tricky year. I was fighting a legal battle, launching a new business, my husband was working away which meant that I was raising two young children on my own. I felt as though I was drowning. Then, just when I thought I couldn't get any lower, a family situation devastated me and I felt broken. I had no fight left. In a relatively short space of time, with Helen's support and listening (not judging and trying to give me advice on what she thought I should do) and by using her amazing therapy techniques and skills, I was soon back on the road to being me again. Friends and family praised me for the strength I showed through these challenges and how quickly I 'bounced back'. I couldn't have managed without Helen by my side supporting me and helping me to become mentally strong in order to get through it all. For this, I am truly grateful.

Susie Sharpe ~ *Owner of Angelic Little Ones*

I have been privileged to know Helen as a friend, therapist and teacher for several years now. She is very caring, honest, helpful and genuine. Personally, I have benefitted greatly from healing sessions with Helen, both on a physical and emotional level and would recommend Helen to anyone seeking help or guidance in any aspect of their life. I have attended various workshops and events that Helen has hosted and her knowledge and understanding of the Spiritual Metaphysical world is amazing. She is ready to give advice and assistance and has answers for all kinds of questions whatever the stage of a person's spiritual journey. Helen is an amazing lady, having all the qualities that equate to a truly genuine gifted healer, teacher and friend.

Sara Jones

I was recommended to Helen at a time when my work was stressful and full of change. After my first visit I immediately found a change in myself, as she helped me with issues that I never realised were affecting me. She has helped me by releasing negative energy and ties. By using techniques that Helen has shown me, I feel better about myself, less stressed and more able to cope with life's trials. I am also more content and happier within myself. She is continuing to help me with my journey. Thank you Helen.

Judy Fowkes

I am so pleased I found Helen Courtney of Evolving You. She is a brilliant therapist and mentor – professional, calm, supportive and very knowledgeable. She has been a major asset on my journey of self-discovery and personal growth. She has many aspects to her therapy, so whatever your issue may be, I totally recommend that you go to see her for a consultation.

Pennie Munslow ~ *Author of 'The Circle of Life'*

I was referred to Helen last year by a very good, close friend of mine. I was looking for spiritual guidance for personal growth with my own personal relationship issues. I found Helen to be very professional, non-judgemental and very easy to communicate with. Helen understood my needs and together we worked through the issues impacting on my life at that time. I would have no hesitation in recommending Helen, especially if you are on a spiritual pathway to enlightenment. Thank you Helen.

Jayne Sheen ~ *Intuitive Holistic Therapist*

Working with Helen has been life-changing! She is someone who you instantly feel comfortable pouring your heart out to, and who you can instantly trust. Her extensive knowledge and approaches are just incredible, as she draws upon exactly what is needed. She is supportive in the healing process and helps you to identify and release what is holding you back, which is very important! She is thorough, caring and compassionate and comes from a place of authenticity and deep care. Helen has been through her own challenges and encourages you to take ownership and responsibility for your own in a supportive and kind-hearted way. She absolutely walks her talk, which is absolutely priceless and I cannot recommend her enough!

Carrie Eddins ~ *www.chocolaterehab.com*

References

New Domestic Abuse Law Could Criminalise 'Psychological Abuse' Of Partners, The Huffington Post UK, 20 August 2014, 28 August 2014, http://www.huffingtonpost.co.uk/2014/08/20/domestic-abuse-law-partners_n_5694055.html

Collins Paperback English Dictionary, Fourth Edition 1999, Glasgow: HarperCollins Publishers

Cyberbullying and Bullying Statistics 2014, Finally!, Nobullying.com, 17 March 2015, 28 August 2015, http://nobullying.com/cyberbullying-bullying-statistics-2014-finally/

Andie Steele Smith, Andie Steele Smith Cyberstalking Victims Resource, 28 August 2014, http://andrewsteelesmith.blogspot.co.uk/p/stalking-victims-resource-uk-stalking_26.html

Katherine Sellgren, BBC News, 8 January 2014, 28 August 2014, http://www.bbc.co.uk/news/education-25639839

Statistics, Living Without Abuse, 28 August 2014, http://www.lwa.org.uk/understanding-abuse/statistics.htm

Russell Myers, Bullies who subject partners to emotional abuse could be jailed under tough new laws, The Mirror, 22 November 2014, 28 November 2014, http://www.mirror.co.uk/news/uk-news/bullies-who-subject-partners-emotional-4677971

Cycle of abuse, Wikipedia, 28 August 2014, 26 March 2015, http://en.wikipedia.org/wiki/Cycle_of_abuse